D1210148

Million Heirs

Million Heirs

John V. Childers, Jr.

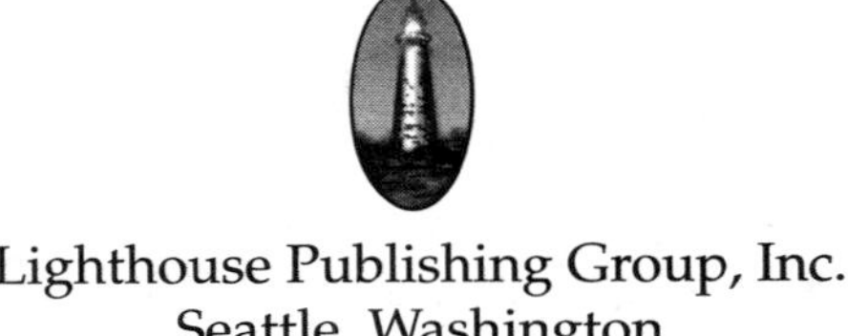

Lighthouse Publishing Group, Inc.
Seattle, Washington

Library of Congress Cataloging-in-Publication Data
Childers, John V., Jr.
Million Heirs/John V. Childers, Jr.
p. cm.
1. Estate Planning--United States--Popular Works 2. I. Title.
KF750.Z9C46 1998
346.7305'2--dc21 98-28110
ISBN 0-910019-76-2

This book is sold with the understanding that neither the author nor the publisher is engaged in rendering legal, accounting, or professional services. Questions relevant to the specific tax, legal, and accounting needs of the reader should be addressed to practicing members of those professions.

The information, ideas, and suggestions contained herein have been developed from sources, including publications and research, that are considered and believed to be reliable, but cannot be guaranteed insofar as they apply to any particular individual. Moreover, because of the technical nature of the material and the fact that laws are never static, but ever changing, the assistance of a competent, qualified lawyer or accountant is recommended when implementing any plans or ideas discussed in this book.

The Author and the Publisher specifically disclaim any liability, loss, or risk, personal or otherwise, incurred as a consequence directly or indirectly of the use and application of any of the techniques or contents of this book.

Lighthouse Publishing would like to acknowledge the following people for their hard work on the creation of this book:
Executive Direction by Cheryle Hamilton
Book Design by Brent Magarrell
Cover Design by Brendan Bigley
Production Direction by Alison Curtis and Mark Engelbrecht
Art Direction by Cynthia Fliege
Marketing by Noel Thomas
Editing/Proofing by Connie Suehiro, Kathleen Thompson, Judy Burkhalter

Published by Lighthouse Publishing Group, Inc.
14675 Interurban Avenue South
Seattle, WA 98168-4664
1-800-706-8657
206-901-3100 (fax)
www.lighthousebooks.com

Source Code: MH98

Printed in the United States of America
10 9 8 7 6 5 4 3 2 1

To my parents,
John and Brenda Childers;

Thanks for making everything possible

Other books by Lighthouse Publishing Group, Inc.

Cook's Book On Creative Real Estate, Wade Cook
How To Pick Up Foreclosures, Wade Cook
Real Estate Money Machine, Wade Cook
Real Estate For Real People, Wade Cook
101 Ways To Buy Real Estate Without Cash, Wade Cook

Bear Market Baloney, Wade Cook
Blueprints For Success, Volume 1, Various Authors
Rolling Stocks, Gregory Witt
Sleeping Like A Baby, John Hudelson
Stock Market Miracles, Wade Cook
Wall Street Money Machine, Wade Cook

Brilliant Deductions, Wade Cook
The Secret Millionaire Guide To Nevada Corporations, John V. Childers, Jr.
Wealth 101, Wade Cook

A+, Wade Cook
Business Buy The Bible, Wade Cook
Don't Set Goals, Wade Cook
Living In Color, Renae Knapp

Contents

Forms

Part I General Information

Part II Items For Immediate Attention

Part III Finances, Assets, and Liabilities

Acknowledgments

ny project as big as writing and assembling a book requires numerous people who provide key assistance and support to make it all happen. Without the following people, this book would never have been completed. I would first like to thank my good friend Johnny Tollett whose vision served as the impetus for this book as well as the service which his company Vantage Planning, LLC provides. There is no way you would be reading this book right now without his and his wife Amber's tireless efforts to get things done. Also from Vantage Planning, LLC, I need to thank my friends Michael Johnson, and Craig and Wendy Lair for everything they have contributed to making this project a reality. As always, I need to thank Alison Curtis and all of the great folks at Lighthouse Publishing for giving me the opportunity to make this information available. Special thanks are also extended to Kathy Voorhees for keeping me on track and not letting me procrastinate too much. I also want to thank my friend and mentor Wade Cook for inspiring me to actually get out and write books and design educational materials rather than simply talk about it.

None of this would be possible without the support and encouragement from my family. I need to give a special thanks to my parents, John and Brenda Childers, who continue to teach me many of the most important things in life. It is because of them that any of this is possible. I'd also like to thank my in-laws, Eddie and Katherine Creighton, for always making me feel special and for giving me the best thing that ever happened to me, my wonderful wife Jill. The support, understanding, and patience she extends are truly more than I deserve and provide the quintessential ingredient in anything I could ever hope or dream to accomplish.

Foreword

nce in awhile, I come across a book which has the potential to forever change the lives of everyone who uses the knowledge and strategies contained therein. As an author of books on many different subjects, I am constantly reading and going through just about anything I can get my hands on. When I found this new book, *Million Heirs*, by my friend John V. Childers, Jr., I knew right away that it had the potential to not only change lives, but to affect fortunes, family dynasties, retirements, and financial destinies.

I have the privilege and opportunity to work with individuals from all over this country, and I am convinced that there is an overall lack of planning. I don't just mean estate planning or tax planning, but a lack of planning in general. I often teach my speakers and team members that we need to constantly strive to help the people of this country to understand how to take care of themselves and their families without relying on others for that assistance. One of the best ways I know to do that is to educate them on some of the issues which too often fall through the cracks in our formalized education process. A phrase I continually use with my team members is, "Get back to the basics." The "basics" are what builds anything worthwhile in this country and it is these financial basics which are spelled out in usable detail in JJ's book.

I honestly believe that people tend to forget what it was that got them to their station in life. I see people all the time who learn simple strategies for doing things, whether it's making money or anything else, but then they stray from these bread and butter skills. I see people who get so excited about the advanced strategies and tactics for how to do things that they forget the basics. In this exciting new book, JJ Childers provides the basic information which is badly needed by today's families.

What excites me so much about *Million Heirs* is that it is a basic "how to" book which will prove to be the most important information you ever deal with. It is a book about taking care of the most important thing in life—your families. Do whatever it takes to obtain and *use* this *Million Heirs*!

Wade B. Cook
New York Times Business Best-Selling Author,
Wall Street Money Machine
Stock Market Miracles
Business Buy The Bible

Preface

In many ways, *Million Heirs* may well be one of the most important books you ever read. This is not so much for what you will learn from the content, but more from what you will accomplish through the use of this book. That's right, the use of this book. Let me explain what I mean by that.

Million Heirs is not designed for your reading pleasure. It is designed to help you in an area where people often find themselves in an utterly confused state. It is a planning guide, but it is also much more than that. It is a book about your life.

That may sound strange to you at first. How on earth could I write a book about you when I don't even know you? The way I'm able to do this is that you will be an associate author. You may never have thought of yourself as an author before, but that is exactly what you will become as you use *Million Heirs*.

With that thought in mind, let's take a closer look at what this book is all about. In order for you to fully understand the purpose of *Million Heirs*, you need to understand how it came about.

One night, I was at a dinner party and I started talking to a friend of mine. The topic of that conversation was a topic I find myself talking about rather frequently: business. It happens that my friend is in a business very similar to mine and we had been thinking along the same lines about a new business idea. Through that conversation, the idea for this book was first developed.

To give you a little background, I am an attorney specializing in the areas of asset protection, estate planning, and tax reduction. I travel throughout the country speaking with people from all walks of life on how they can preserve more of the wealth that they have spent their lives accumulating. Additionally, I spend a great deal of my time developing products that outline exactly how individuals can accomplish these important objectives. Along these lines, I had recently been thinking about developing a new product.

I mentioned the idea to my friend who is in a similar business. He is a certified public accountant (CPA) specializing in the area of taxation. He deals with small business owners and others who have created large amounts of wealth on a regular basis. With this background, he had identified an important need of these individuals and had been heavily involved in forming a business to address that need.

During our conversation, he told me that he was well into the process of developing that new business with a couple of our mutual friends. In outlining the concept behind their business, I realized that we were on the same page, so to speak, in our thinking. I told him a little bit about what I had been working toward and we came to an agreement. It was time to form an alliance.

Million Heirs is a product of that alliance. It is the first portion of a package designed to assist you immensely with an area of crucial significance to you and your loved ones. The idea behind this program is simple. Relaying important information about oneself is too often overlooked. In fact, you yourself may have overlooked this important area. To make that determination, you need to ask yourself a few simple questions.

If your father/mother passed away today, would you know how to take care of all of their affairs? If you think you can, take a closer look by asking yourself a few more in depth questions like:

- Do you know whether or not they owe anyone any money? If they do, how much?
- Do you know whether or not anyone owes them any money? If so, how much?
- Are they involved in any business transactions or investments which owe them money?
- What types of bank accounts or brokerage accounts do they have and where are they?
- How much money is in each of these accounts? How do you know?
- Is there any money and/or other valuables hidden in a special area? If so, where is it?
- Is there anyone who needs to be contacted? If so, who? When?
- What type of estate planning is in place?
- What is involved in the handling of their estate?
- What type of financial situation are they in?
- Do they have money in retirement accounts? If so, where? How much?
- Do they have insurance? If so, how much? What type? Who is it with? Who are the beneficiaries of the policy?
- How much are the items in their estate worth?

Are you beginning to get the picture? Some of you reading this may think that you know the answers to these questions. Let me ask you another important question. Are you sure?

You see, too many times people find themselves in a lost world when it comes to this issue. Estate planning is certainly about wills, trusts, insurance, and other instruments, but it is also about planning things which may seem quite simple and mundane, yet prove to be the most difficult of all.

When I first started thinking about this, I put myself to the test. Being an estate planning lawyer, I probably knew more about my parents' situation than most but it terrified me to think about all of the horrible consequences which I might face without proper planning. Perhaps the most frightening thing is that the vast majority of individuals will never do anything about recording the information they'll need after a loved one passes on.

I started thinking about times when my parents told me to check through everything with a fine-toothed comb before I got rid of it. I distinctly remember an instance when my father told me about one thousand dollars which was hidden in a secret compartment of his desk. What would happen if I forgot about this and sold the desk for $300? Someone would get a great deal, that's for sure. It's also sure that it wouldn't be me.

You may be thinking that all you need to do is to sit down and talk about things and you will simply remember it all. Folks, you may have a good memory but memory alone is not a plan. Memories tend to fade. Besides that, your thinking doesn't tend to work as clearly when you find yourself in a situation where you've lost a loved one.

Million Heirs is assembled to assist you tremendously when you find yourself in this type of situation. I have set forth specific areas of concern which will need to be addressed when that time comes. I have also gone to great lengths to include all of those items which tend to be forgotten during stressful times surrounding loss.

Let me assure you, this is no small undertaking. People often neglect to pay attention to some of the smallest, yet most important issues. That's where *Million Heirs* comes in. To give you a sense of what those items might entail, ask yourself the following questions:

If your father/mother passed away today, would you know:

- Where they would like to be buried?
- If they would like to be buried rather than other options?
- Where they would like their funeral to be held?
- How they would like the funeral to be organized?
- Who they would want to give the eulogy?
- What songs they would like as a part of the funeral?

The questions which must be answered go on and on. The sad reality is that everyday, hundreds of people find themselves in situations where they do not know how to handle necessary decisions because they didn't prepare ahead of time.

You may find yourself in a situation right now where your parents are already deceased. You may remember how difficult the process was when you went through it, but now it's over. You may feel that you have things covered. However, I want you to think about something a little differently. You know the confusion which accompanies the inability to answer the previous questions? How does that feel? Think about it.

Now ask yourself exactly how your family would handle things in the event that you were to pass away tomorrow. Would they be able to answer all of the questions I posed earlier? Have you left them properly equipped?

Chances are, you are no better prepared than the majority of people who fail to plan. Even though you've purchased the insurance, structured your will and/or trusts, you still haven't taken care of some of the most important details. The key now is to determine how to take control over the situation. The simple truth is, if you don't take control of the situation, the situation will take control of you.

Once you decide to gain control, it's time to take action. I mentioned earlier that *Million Heirs* is the first part of the overall program. Through the use of this book, you will equip yourself and your family with the tools needed to deal with difficult times. *Million Heirs* will play a central role in getting you started in the right direction.

The next part of the program is to get assistance. I told you earlier about my friend with whom I formed this powerful business alliance. His vision was to design a company which would take the headaches out of estate preparation. His company, Vantage Planning, LLC, provides a service where vital records are kept for family members and where many of the difficult tasks surrounding death are handled in a way which enables the family more flexibility to deal with the issues surrounding unfortunate times.

Through this business, families are able to provide detailed instructions for handling their affairs when they're gone. Parents are able to structure things in a way which takes a great deal of stress out of the entire scenario. By using *Million Heirs* and the services provided by Vantage Planning, LLC, parents are able to outline exactly how things should function. A brief description of Vantage Planning, LLC and the services which they provide are included in the section entitled Additional Resources, located at the back of this book.

Everything included in this book is designed with the idea of creating a plan for you and your family. Too many times, these plans are never designed. The problem is that people are always aiming to get around to it. People think that they will take care of things "later." In the real world, however, "later" can come much sooner than you realize.

No matter how much time you spend on becoming successful, you must make sure you avoid becoming a failure. What I mean by this is that you must have a plan. Because when all is said and done, *if you fail to plan, you plan to fail!*

Part I
General Information

The first type of information which needs to be gathered is quite basic, but it is also often overlooked. Much of the personal information you take for granted is not common knowledge to those closest to you. For instance, do you know your spouse's Social Security number? How about his or her driver's license number? Do your kids know yours? You see, general information such as your address, phone number, Social Security number, and date of birth should be documented not only as it applies to you, but also to your spouse, your children, and perhaps even your grandchildren. The General Information section contains input forms to record this information.

Perhaps the most important information you can document for your loved ones are the names and phone numbers of your personal and professional contacts and advisors. Too many times, individuals tend to forget about those who will be playing a key role in the handling of their estates and the accompanying circumstances. You need to put together a list of all the key players in your estate. Having this valuable resource close at hand could prove invaluable to those who will eventually have to close your estate.

You may think that this is a simple matter because there really aren't that many people involved, but you could be quite surprised. Think about all the people who are involved in your day-to-day affairs. The following is just a short list of some of the central figures.

Minister/Rabbi/Priest: Many people tend to forget to include instructions for how they want their funeral handled. What's more, they forget to tell who they want to preside over the ceremony. Your personal or family minister is most likely the one who will be asked to do the eulogy at your funeral. For this reason, it is crucial to have this information available for those you leave behind.

Insurance Agent: Your insurance agent will undoubtedly need to be contacted in order to access your life insurance information. In many instances, family members may not be familiar with who provides your insurance. It may be a close friend of yours, but your children may have never met this person. Additionally, as you will see while assembling this information, there could be several individuals who would need to be contacted regarding life or accidental death insurance.

Attorney: The role of your attorney(s) is a matter of great importance in settling your estate. Your attorney(s) will have all relevant information regarding your will, trusts, estate plans, pending legal matters, and other vital records and documents. Because they play such a large part in this process, it is especially important to document all names, numbers, and addresses.

Accountant: The role of the accountant in the estate settlement process is extremely important. Upon your death, there are a number of issues which must be addressed regarding your tax situation. Your accountant will have copies of all previously filed income tax returns, as well as pertinent tax strategies you have put into practice.

Stockbroker: Many times, individuals may have established investment and trading accounts that others are not aware of. Your broker will have information on your investment portfolio. However, this does you no good whatsoever unless you list the name of each broker and how to get into contact with them.

Financial Planner: A profession which plays a larger part today than ever before in the estate planning and financial planning process is the financial planner. Your personal financial planner will have details on all of your investments, retirement plans, insurance policies, and estate plans.

Realtor: Your realtor could be needed in the event your heirs wish to sell your current home. In many instances, this becomes increasingly important in order to satisfy any obligations surrounding the estate. It can save a lot of time, effort, energy, and even money, by having the name of a trusted advisor to assist in this matter rather than searching for just anyone.

Doctor: Upon the death of an individual, various records are needed for many different purposes. One set of these records is those documenting your medical history. Medical records can be required for many different reasons, including insurance. Your medical specialists will have your medical history documented and can provide this information upon demand. These medical specialists can include, but are not limited to, your family practitioner, dentist, pediatrician, OB/GYN, and ophthalmologist.

Veterinarian: Your veterinarian will have shot records and medical information on your pets. This may not seem necessary, but can be quite helpful when folks pass away and leave pets behind for family members to take care of.

This is but a small listing of the various individuals who will play a key role in the overall handling of your estate. Input forms for the contacts and advisors listed above, as well as space for other contacts, can be found in the following pages. Be sure to fill these out completely and to keep them up to date as the years go by.

Family Information

	You	Spouse
Name	____________	____________
Address	____________	____________
Street/PO Box	____________	____________
City/State	____________	____________
Zip Code	____________	____________
Phone #	____________	____________
Social Security #	____________	____________
Date of Birth	____________	____________
Place of Birth	____________	____________
Occupation	____________	____________
Place of Employment		
Company Name	____________	____________
Street/PO Box	____________	____________
	____________	____________
City/State	____________	____________
Zip Code	____________	____________
Employer's Phone #	____________	____________
Driver's License #	____________	____________
Parent's name	____________	____________
Parent's phone #	____________	____________

General Information

	Child 1	Child 2
Name		
Address		
Street/PO Box		
City/State		
Zip Code		
Phone #		
Social Security #		
Date of Birth		
Place of Birth		
Parent's Name		

	Child 3	Child 4
Name		
Address		
Street/PO Box		
City/State		
Zip Code		
Phone #		
Social Security #		
Date of Birth		
Place of Birth		
Parent's Name		

For additional children, reference Notes on Pages 14-16.

Extended Family Information

	Grandchild 1	Grandchild 2
Name		
Address		
Street/PO Box		
City/State		
Zip Code		
Phone #		
Social Security #		
Date of Birth		
Place of Birth		
Parent's Name		

	Grandchild 3	Grandchild 4
Name		
Address		
Street/PO Box		
City/State		
Zip Code		
Phone #		
Social Security #		
Date of Birth		
Place of Birth		
Parent's Name		

General Information

	Grandchild 5	Grandchild 6
Name		
Address		
Street/PO Box		
City/State		
Zip Code		
Phone #		
Social Security #		
Date of Birth		
Place of Birth		
Parent's Name		

	Grandchild 7	Grandchild 8
Name		
Address		
Street/PO Box		
City/State		
Zip Code		
Phone #		
Social Security #		
Date of Birth		
Place of Birth		
Parent's Name		

For additional children, reference Notes on Pages 14-16.

Personal Contacts/Advisors

	Name	Business Name
Minister	____________	____________
Insurance Agent - 1	____________	____________
Insurance Agent - 2	____________	____________
Insurance Agent - 3	____________	____________
Attorney	____________	____________
Accountant	____________	____________
Stockbroker	____________	____________
Financial Planner	____________	____________
Realtor	____________	____________

General Information

Address	Phone #

Personal Contacts/Advisors (continued)

	Name	Business Name
Family Practitioner	________________	________________
Dentist	________________	________________
Pediatrician	________________	________________
OB/GYN	________________	________________
Opthamologist	________________	________________
Other Specialist - 1	________________	________________
Other Specialist - 2	________________	________________
Other Specialist - 3	________________	________________
Veterinarian	________________	________________

General Information

Address	Phone #

Other Contacts/Advisors

(You fill in the blanks)	Name	Business Name

General Information

Address	Phone #

Notes

Notes

Notes

Part II
Items For Immediate Attention

o matter how well you plan for your eventual death, your heirs will not be prepared for the initial items that must be tended to immediately following your passing. They will not have the mindset to handle all of the things that will come up. In the following section, Items for Immediate Attention, you have the opportunity to document the information your family will need to help ensure a more organized transition in the days immediately following your death.

Undoubtedly, you and your family have numerous relatives and friends that will need to be notified of this unfortunate event. Documenting exactly who these individuals are and how they can be contacted can take care of an enormous amount of work for your family, leaving one less task for them to be burdened with. It would also be helpful to designate one person to contact these individuals or perhaps, to arrange a calling tree where the tedious effort of locating these individuals is not placed on your family in their time of grief. This can take care of what would otherwise be a lot of work for one person.

In most instances, families are simply unaware of the amount of information which must be dealt with. The number of items which must be taken care of in this difficult time is astounding. For instance, if you do have burial insurance, this information needs to be readily available for your family. Burial insurance policies are generally only $500 with no cash surrender value. The face amounts of the various policies are used directly against services and merchandise. Additionally, if you have a burial insurance policy, someone needs to contact the seller of the policy before burial. In some instances, burial policies can be null and void or only partially redeemable if the issuing company is not notified before burial. This is important information which needs to be documented for your family.

The more your family knows about you, the better shape they will be in upon your death. For this reason, let's take a look at the subject of burial policies in a bit more detail.

Burial policies are generally purchased through a funeral home. Many people falsely believe that they have a burial insurance policy when, in fact, what they really have is only a life insurance policy. While funeral homes are the primary source of burial policies, similar policies can be purchased through your insurance agent. If you are in the market for a burial policy, it would be a good idea to find out exactly what type of insurance policy you are about to purchase and then shop around with other insurance agents.

It is important to note that life insurance policies from other insurance companies can be assigned directly to funeral homes to pay for the funeral. Your insurance company will need a certified death certificate, a copy of the funeral charges, and the beneficiary's signature.

One of the biggest problems surrounding the death of a loved one is the shock at how much money is involved in laying the deceased to rest. The cost of a funeral can accumulate quickly. Too often, families find themselves in a situation which they are completely unprepared for, not only from an emotional standpoint, but from an economic aspect as well.

An item which must be considered in preparing your estate for your family is the overall cost and planning involved in a funeral. I have gathered information on the various expenses involved and have compiled a list of charges and approximate costs of the typical funeral. Obviously, these amounts may not be specific to your area but are somewhat indicative of the national average.

The costs stated below represent a guide to better enable you to understand exactly what expenses are involved. Please consult your local funeral home to get exact quotes on what they would charge you for similar services.

Casket: Caskets can run anywhere from $400 for a cloth covered wood casket to as much as $7,500 for a full couch solid bronze casket.

Funeral Home Service: These charges include, but are not limited to staff assistance, phone answering, filing of the death certificate, and preparation of registry books. The average cost is around $950.

Embalming: The average cost of embalming is around $500.

Body Preparation: This includes cosmetics and other types of preparation for viewing. The typical cost for this service is around $75 to $100.

Visitation Services: The average cost associated with visitation services is approximately $200.

Transfer of Body to Funeral Home: General transfer fees run around $200.

Hearse: The typical expense of renting the hearse is $100.

Church or Chapel Service: This is generally around $400.

Graveside Service: This expense is typically $175.

Family Car: A separate car is often provided for members of the family to ride in together at a cost of $35.

Pall Bearer Car: A separate vehicle for pall bearers is generally $30.

Flower Van: The approximate cost for this service is $30.

Opening and Closing of Grave: The cost for this service is around $200.

Tent Setup: This tends to cost around $100.

Miscellaneous Expenses: These expenses include registration books, memorial folders, thank you notes, temporary grave markers, and boutonnieres for pall bearers. The average expense for this is between $45 and $75.

Death Certificates: This cost will vary depending on state regulations. However, the cost will be approximately $4 for the original and $1 for each additional copy.

Burial Plot: Obviously, this will vary from place to place, but the cost is generally from $200 to $500.

Steel or Concrete Box: Some cemeteries require boxes in order to keep the ground level. This can cost about $350.

Steel or Concrete Vault: Depending upon how elaborate you get, the cost for this can range anywhere from a low of $700 to as high as $10,000.

Tombstone: The cost of the tombstone can vary significantly depending on how elaborate it is. The cost can run anywhere from $2,000 to $10,000.

Sales Tax: Since a service is being provided and a sale is taking place, the government also participates in this process by adding a sales tax to all of the above expenses. The amount of this tax will vary by state.

Obviously, the cost of a funeral cannot be overlooked in planning for your eventual death. In fact, most funeral homes offer prearranged funeral packages where you can purchase your funeral at today's prices. If you are young, this could be a worthwhile investment. At a minimum, it takes much of the burden off of your survivors. Please consult your local funeral home and your financial planner to see what option is best suited for your specific situation.

Another important step that will need to be addressed immediately is your preferred funeral arrangements. There are many different questions which must be answered. The biggest problem is that people forget to think about these questions and leave their families to try to answer them. By considering the various decisions which must be made beforehand, you can take a large step toward leaving your family in a much better situation. For example, consider the following questions:

- What funeral home do you wish to use?
- Do you wish to use a specific funeral director?
- Do you own a burial plot?
- In what cemetery is your burial plot located?
- If you don't have a burial plot, in what cemetery do you wish to be buried?
- Is there a specific church or facility where you would like your funeral held?

These are but a few of the many questions which must be answered. If this information is not documented somewhere, it is a safe bet that your heirs will not know how to answer these important questions when they have to.

One of the most difficult tasks surrounding the death of a loved one is planning the funeral. This is because much of the planning surrounding your funeral will be a matter of preference. For instance, certain individuals do not wish to have flowers sent to their funeral. If this happens to be your intent, one option would be to have donations sent to a specific charitable organization in lieu of flowers. Is this something that others would know? Which particular charity would you prefer? You must make your intentions known.

It is also important for your family to know if you wish to be an organ donor. This information is usually found on your driver's license, but it is a good idea to document it in case your driver's license cannot be found or you do not have one.

In addition to your driver's license, certain vital personal documents need to be available to your family for specific situations. These items include birth certificates, marriage licenses, your living will, durable power of attorney, will, codicil(s), and trust documents. These documents serve specific purposes and will need to be accessed by your heirs. These documents and their locations should be documented and kept up to date on the forms included in this section.

The information in this section, while difficult to deal with now, will save your family time and problems in the period immediately following your death. It will alleviate the burden of having to track down this information, and give them more time to concentrate on the important matters that will soon come up.

Items For Immediate Attention

People to be Contacted Immediately

Name	Phone #	Relationship

Million Heirs

People to be Contacted Immediately

Name	Phone #	Relationship

Items For Immediate Attention

People to be Contacted Immediately

Name	Phone #	Relationship

Burial Insurance

Do you have burial insurance? _____ Yes _____ No

If yes, please complete below section.

Amount of policy ____

Insurance company ____

Agent's Name ____

Phone # ____

Does your spouse have burial insurance? _____ Yes _____ No

If yes, please complete below section.

Amount of policy ____

Insurance company ____

Agent's Name ____

Phone # ____

Items For Immediate Attention

Funeral Arrangements

Do you want to be cremated? _____ Yes _____ No

Funeral Home ______________________________

Funeral Director ______________________________

Phone # ______________________________

Cemetery Name ______________________________

Location (City/State) ______________________________

Phone # ______________________________

Other Specifics About Your Funeral?

Do you want flowers? _____ Yes _____ No

Donations to charitable organizations? _____ Yes _____ No

If yes, please list below.

____

____

____

Other

____

Organ Donation

Do you wish to be an organ donor? _____ Yes _____ No

If yes, please see below.

Is this noted on your driver's license? _____ Yes _____ No

Have you filled out an organ donor card? _____ Yes _____ No

If yes, where is it located? ____

Vital Record Locations

	Location	Phone #	Contact
Birth Certificate	____________________	____________	_______________
Marriage License	____________________	____________	_______________
Prearranged funeral plan	____________________	____________	_______________
Living Will	____________________	____________	_______________
Durable Power of Attorney	____________________	____________	_______________
Wills/Codicil	____________________	____________	_______________
Trust Documents	____________________	____________	_______________

Items For Immediate Attention

Obituary

Do you have a prepared obituary? _____ Yes _____ No

If yes, please write below.

If more space is required, please see Notes on pages 29-30.

Epitaph

Do you have a prepared epitaph? _____ Yes _____ No

If yes, please write below.

____

____

____

____

____

____

____

____

____

____

____

____

____

____

____

If more space is required, please see Notes on pages 29-30.

Items For Immediate Attention

Notes

Notes

Part III

Finances, Assets, and Liabilities

inancial information is typically the most difficult information to gather upon the death of a loved one. Oftentimes, one person controls a family's finances. While one spouse might know that the other spouse has some life insurance, retirement plans, savings accounts, et cetera, he or she probably could not sit and tell you what assets, liabilities, income, and expenses make up their family's financial portfolio. It is crucial that you take the time to document this important information.

While it would seem obvious to many people that important financial information needs to be documented, most people never actually get around to it. Perhaps if they realized how expensive it can be to fail to make this documentation they would pay it greater attention. It has been estimated that there is over $5,000,000,000 in unclaimed assets waiting to be claimed by rightful heirs. In most cases, the surviving family members did not know these assets ever existed. These assets include:

- Checking, savings, and brokerage accounts
- Stocks and bonds
- Life and accidental death insurance policies
- Safe deposit boxes
- Partnerships and business interests

It is extremely important that you take the time to structure what is referred to as a personal inventory of all your assets. This list will include many different types of information. Be sure to fill this section accurately and completely and keep it updated.

If you're like most people, the idea of taking a personal inventory of your assets and liabilities to distribute to family members has crossed your mind.

The truth is, most people are very uncomfortable when it comes to planning for their death. Nevertheless, this planning or inventory of personal information is an extremely important step to assure that your family has the resources it needs to meet the constant demands of life.

Have you ever sat down and thought about how much viable information you would want your family to know if something were to happen to you? You probably don't realize just how overwhelming this information is. The number of questions which must be answered is absolutely mind-boggling. The hardest part of all of this is that the situation only gets worse when it has to be dealt with upon the death of a family member. Consider the following:

- Have you opened a separate savings account for a rainy day?
- Does your family know about it?
- Who should your spouse or family contact to access your retirement plans?
- Does your family know of the safe deposit box you have just opened?
- How much life insurance do you have?
- Do you have any accidental death insurance?

A problem which often arises is that family members are not aware of benefits which may be available. For instance, it is quite common for automotive insurance policies, bank accounts, and credit cards to carry a small amount of accidental death insurance on its customers. Is this true in your situation? If so, would the people you are closest to have knowledge of this information? This section, Finances, Assets, and Liabilities, contains detailed information on practically all aspects of your family's financial portfolio. I strongly recommend that you look over these input forms, fill them out thoroughly, and review them every three to six months to see what changes need to be made.

Detailed information including dollar amounts, account numbers, and contact phone numbers will prove to be an invaluable resource to your family. Items that need to be documented include:

- Current sources of income, both monthly and annually
- Current liabilities and expenses
- Bank accounts
- Credit cards
- Brokerage accounts
- Investments in real estate
- Safe deposit boxes
- Creditors

- Debtors
- Business interests
- Retirement plans
- Insurance policies

While this is by no means an all-inclusive list of everything associated with your finances, assets, and liabilities, you can begin to see the point. I know that I have stated it several times already, but I do believe that taking action is the key to your overall success. Although compiling much of this information could be very time consuming, the resulting resource will be an asset that your family cannot do without.

Current Sources of Income

	Description
Employment - 1	
Employment - 2	
Employment Spouse - 1	
Employment Spouse - 2	
Independent Contractor	
Independent Contractor - Spouse	
Pension	
Pension - Spouse	
Annuity	
Rental Income - 1	
Rental Income - 2	
Rental Income - 3	

Finances, Assets, and Liabilities

Annual Amount	Payment Frequency	Phone Number

Current Sources of Income (continued)

	Description
Royalties	______________________
Interest	______________________
Dividends	______________________
Trust Fund	______________________
Alimony	______________________
Child Support	______________________
Notes Receivable - 1	______________________
Notes Receivable - 2	______________________
Legal Settlement	______________________
Insurance Settlement	______________________
Other - 1	______________________
Other - 2	______________________

Finances, Assets, and Liabilities

Annual Amount	Payment Frequency	Phone Number

Bank Accounts

Bank Name	Type	Account #

Finances, Assets, and Liabilities

Location	Phone #	Average Balance

Credit Card Accounts

Name	Type	Account #

Finances, Assets, and Liabilities

Phone #	Unpaid Balance	Accumulated Benefits

Brokerage/Investment Accounts

Institution Name	Contact

Real Estate Owned

Location	Mortgage Holder	Unpaid Balance

Finances, Assets, and Liabilities

Phone #	Type of Account	Average Balance

Monthly Payment	Market Value	Annual Rentals

Safe Deposit Boxes

Institution Name	Branch Location

Debtors

Name	Unpaid Balance	Monthly Payment

Finances, Assets, and Liabilities

Box #	Signatures on Account

Secured By	Interest Rate	Phone #

Creditors

	Creditor	Account #
Mortgage - 1	______________	______________
Mortgage - 2	______________	______________
Mortgage - 3	______________	______________
Home Equity	______________	______________
Auto Loan - 1	______________	______________
Auto Loan - 2	______________	______________
Auto Loan - 3	______________	______________
Student Loan - 1	______________	______________
Student Loan - 2	______________	______________
Personal - 1	______________	______________
Personal - 2	______________	______________

Finances, Assets, and Liabilities

Phone #	Unpaid Balance	Monthly Payment	Interest

Creditors (continued)

	Creditor	Account #
Credit Card - 1		
Credit Card - 2		
Credit Card - 3		
Credit Card - 4		
Credit Card - 5		
Credit Card - 6		
Credit Card - 7		
Other		
Other		
Other		
Other		

Finances, Assets, and Liabilities

Phone #	Unpaid Balance	Monthly Payment	Interest

Business Interests

Business Name

Type (Individual, Partnership, Corporation, et cetera)

Percentage Owned

Value of Interest

Buy/Sell Agreement (Y/N and Location)

Business Name

Type (Individual, Partnership, Corporation, et cetera)

Percentage Owned

Value of Interest

Buy/Sell Agreement (Y/N and Location)

Business Name

Type (Individual, Partnership, Corporation, et cetera)

Percentage Owned

Value of Interest

Buy/Sell Agreement (Y/N and Location)

Business Name

Type (Individual, Partnership, Corporation, et cetera)

Percentage Owned

Value of Interest

Buy/Sell Agreement (Y/N and Location)

Finances, Assets, and Liabilities

Retirement Plans

Plan Type	Employer/Holder	Phone #	Value

Current Monthly Income

	$'s
Salary - 1	
Salary - 2	
Salary Spouse - 1	
Salary Spouse - 2	
Independent Contractor	
Independent Contractor - Spouse	
Pension	
Pension - Spouse	
Annuity	
Rental Income - 1	
Rental Income - 2	
Rental Income - 3	

	$'s
Royalties	
Interest	
Dividends	
Trust Fund	
Alimony	
Child Support	
Notes Receivable - 1	
Notes Receivable - 2	
Legal Settlement	
Insurance Settlement	
Other - 1	
Other - 2	

Current Monthly Expenses

	$'s		$'s
Mortgage Payment - 1	________	Auto Insurance	________
Mortgage Payment - 2	________	Electricity	________
Mortgage Payment - 3	________	Gas	________
Rent	________	Telephone	________
Auto Payment - 1	________	Water	________
Auto Payment - 2	________	Cable	________
Auto Payment - 3	________	Child Care	________
Student Loan - 1	________	Other - 1	________
Student Loan - 2	________	Other - 2	________
Credit Card Payments	________	Other - 3	________
Health Insurance	________	Other - 4	________
Life Insurance	________	Other - 5	________

Insurance Policies

Type of Policy	Insurance Company	Agent

Finances, Assets, and Liabilities

Phone #	Face Amount	Cash Value	Beneficiary

Notes

Notes

Notes

Part IV
Personal Possessions

Have you ever thought about what would happen to your possessions when you die? What would happen to your furniture, hardware equipment, collectible items, or even your pots and pans? Many people store up possessions over many years and these assets can have emotional or financial value. It is important that you document all of your personal assets.

Look around your house and complete the forms in this section. As you list all your possessions, you also need to decide what the present value of each item is and who you would like to receive the item. As you'll see on the following input forms, the rooms in your home have been divided with applicable items listed, including your garage, basement, and attic.

There is also additional space available to list items that were not included in the room by room detail of your home. For example, your dining room chairs and table may be worth $1,500 and you may want your sister to have them. This needs to be documented. Listing all of your items might be time consuming, but it will definitely benefit your heirs and prevent potential hardships for families during a period when tensions are already high. Documenting and maintaining this information is absolutely essential.

Your financial and informational records are a very important piece of your life puzzle. Having this information readily available for your heirs can benefit them greatly. These documents are important, be sure to spend the required time organizing their whereabouts.

One common cause of people failing to properly organize these records is that they fail to understand why they are needed. For example, why would your heirs need to know where your current and past income tax statements are located? Even when you die, the government still wants its part of what you made during that year. Past income statements would give your heirs an idea of what to look for in the area of income, deductions, credits, and business expenses.

Additionally, if you die and your spouse applies for a loan, he or she will need tax statements to include in the application. Another factor is that, after your death, the IRS may still audit your past tax statements. Therefore, it is a good idea for your heirs to keep your tax statements for a minimum of six years.

Before you complete the forms in this section, I want to take a little time to answer a couple of questions which often come up. By taking a look at these questions, you will get a better handle on the type of information which is often overlooked so that you will not make the same mistakes.

What Personal and/or Home Services Need to be Discontinued?

This question is one which often goes unnoticed. This section of input forms is designed to assist your family in recognizing what day-to-day expenses and services you incur. These items can be easily overlooked in settling the loved one's financial affairs. As you'll see, many services will need to be discontinued or, in some cases, continued under a different name. For example, if you die, your family would need to cancel your newspaper and magazine subscriptions. They may need to cancel some of your utilities, such as cable or even a house cleaning service. These products or services are things that your family could easily overlook. Unfortunately, they are usually noticed when the issuing company or organization looks to your heirs for payment. Be sure to list all relevant information on the accompanying forms so that your family is prepared.

What Personal Identification Numbers, Combinations, and/or Passwords do you Need to Leave Behind?

Personal identification numbers, passwords, and combinations fill almost every aspect of our financial world. Unfortunately, people typically fail to provide this information to their heirs. In this section, you are given the opportunity to document the passwords you use to get access to your bank card, your home safe, or even your computer. Since this information is extremely confidential, you should consider detailing this information elsewhere, and storing it in a secure location, such as a safe deposit box. If you choose to document this information in this manner, list the location of your personal identification numbers, passwords, and combinations in the personal documents and records section of the related input forms.

Giving your family access to your numbers and/or passwords can be extremely important. In one instance, family members went to the home of their deceased brother to begin sorting through all of his financial information. They had the key to the house, but once they opened the door, the security alarm went off and they did not know the code. This may not be the end of the world, but it is certainly an inconvenience. You can imagine some of the problems which can arise when this information is not provided. The world we live in, surrounded by the need for passwords and other types of identification information, makes it more important than ever to document this sensitive data.

By providing thorough and up to date information about your possessions, you can save your family additional frustration caused by their inability to perform the simplest of tasks, such as signing onto a computer or looking in your briefcase. While documenting this information may seem time-consuming and monotonous, it will prove essential in assisting your heirs.

Personal Assets

	Description	Value	Beneficiary
ATV			
Automobile - 1			
Automobile - 2			
Automobile - 3			
Boat			
Computer			
Jet Ski			
Motorcycle			
Motor Home/RV			
Plane			
Snowmobile			
Other			
Other			
Other			
Other			

Home Inventory - Living Room

	Description	Value	Beneficiary
Chairs			
Clocks			
Coffee Table			
Computer			
Couch/Love Seat			
Entertainment Center			
Drapes			
Lamps			
Mirrors			
Organ/Piano			
Rug - Oriental/Other			
Stereo/Radio			
TV/VCR			
Other			
Other			

Home Inventory - Kitchen

	Description	Value	Beneficiary
China			
Crystal			
Dishes			
Dishwasher			
Freezer			
Glassware			
Hutch			
Microwave			
Pots/Pans			
Refrigerator			
Silverware/Flatware			
Stove			
Wine Rack			
Other			
Other			

Personal Possessions

Home Inventory - Dining Room

	Description	Value	Beneficiary
Buffet			
Bureau			
Centerpieces			
Chairs			
China Cabinet			
Coffee/Tea Service			
Dining Table			
Drapes			
Rug - Oriental/Other			
Serving Table			
Other			
Other			
Other			
Other			
Other			

Home Inventory - Master Bedroom

	Description	Value	Beneficiary
Bed			
Chest			
Comforter			
Curtains			
Dresser			
Mattress			
Night Stand			
Rug			
Trunk and Contents			
TV/VCR			
Vanity			
Other			
Other			
Other			
Other			

Personal Possessions

Home Inventory - Nursery

	Description	Value	Beneficiary
Bassinet	______	______	______
Bookcase	______	______	______
Books	______	______	______
Changing Table	______	______	______
Chest	______	______	______
Crib	______	______	______
Curtains	______	______	______
Lamp	______	______	______
Rocking Chair	______	______	______
Stroller	______	______	______
Swing	______	______	______
Other	______	______	______
Other	______	______	______
Other	______	______	______
Other	______	______	______

Home Inventory - Bedroom 1

	Description	Value	Beneficiary
Bed			
Chest			
Comforter			
Curtains			
Dresser			
Mattress			
Night Stand			
Rug			
TV/VCR			
Other			
Other			
Other			
Other			
Other			
Other			

Personal Possessions

Home Inventory - Bedroom 2

	Description	Value	Beneficiary
Bed			
Chest			
Comforter			
Curtains			
Dresser			
Mattress			
Night Stand			
Rug			
TV/VCR			
Other			
Other			
Other			
Other			
Other			
Other			

Home Inventory - Bedroom 3

	Description	Value	Beneficiary
Bed			
Chest			
Comforter			
Curtains			
Dresser			
Mattress			
Night Stand			
Rug			
TV/VCR			
Other			
Other			
Other			
Other			
Other			
Other			

Personal Possessions

Home Inventory - Garage/Basement/Attic

	Description	Value	Beneficiary
Clothes Dryer			
Hand Tools			
Gardening Tools			
Lawn Mower			
Leaf Blower			
Mulcher			
Power Tools			
Trimmer/Edger			
Washing Machine			
Weed Eater			
Workbench			
Other			
Other			
Other			
Other			

Home Inventory - Sports Equipment

	Description	Value	Beneficiary
Camping Equipment			
Exercise Equipment			
Fishing Equipment			
Golf Clubs			
Ping-pong Table			
Pool Table			
Scuba Gear			
Snow Skis			
Snowboard			
Surfboard			
Tennis equipment			
Water skis			
Weights/Accessories			
Other			
Other			

Personal Possessions

Home Inventory - Miscellaneous

	Description	Value	Beneficiary
Artwork - 1			
Artwork - 2			
Artwork - 3			
Bookcase			
Collections - Coin			
Collections - Sports Cards			
Collections - Stamp			
Collections - Other			
Furs			
Jewelry - 1			
Jewelry - 2			
Jewelry - 3			
Luggage			
Office Machines - 1			
Office Machines - 2			

Home Inventory - Miscellaneous

	Description	Value	Beneficiary
Patio Furniture			
Video Camera			
Sewing Machine			
Other			
Other			
Other			
Other			
Other			
Other			
Other			
Other			
Other			
Other			
Other			
Other			

Personal Possessions

Document Locations

	Location
Current Income Tax Information	
Past Income Tax Returns	
Will	
Safe Deposit Box and Key	
Bank Passbook	
Records of Your T-Bills and CDs	
Records of Money Market/Mutual Funds	
Records of your pension, IRA, Keogh	
Social Security Records	
Veterans Records	
Insurance Policies	
Deeds of Trust	
Records of Stocks and Bonds	

Document Locations

	Location
Records of Loans Owed to You	
Records of Loans You Owe	
Business Records/Contracts	
Real Estate Records	
Auto Ownership Records	
Warranties	
Birth Certificates	
Passports	
Burial Contract	
Funeral Contract	
Other	
Other	
Other	

Personal Possessions

Personal/Home Services to be Discontinued

Discontinued Service	Company Name	Phone #
Cable		
Cellular		
Credit Cards (refer to page 46)		
Country Club Membership		
Electric		
Gas		
Health Club Membership		
Internet Service		
Lawn Service		
Magazines - 1		
Magazines - 2		
Magazines - 3		
Maid Service		

Personal/Home Services to be Discontinued

Discontinued Service	Company Name	Phone #
Newspaper - 1		
Newspaper - 2		
Pool Service		
Satellite		
Trash		
Tree/Shrub Service		
Telephone		
Water		
Other		
Other		
Other		
Other		
Other		

Personal Possessions

PIN Numbers/Combinations/Passwords

	Number/Combination/Password
Bankcard - 1	
Bankcard - 2	
Briefcase	
Car Alarm	
Combination lock - 1	
Combination lock - 2	
Combination lock - 3	
Computer program - 1	
Computer program - 2	
Computer program - 3	
Employee ID#	
House Alarm	
House Safe	

PIN Numbers/Combinations/Passwords

	Number/Combination/Password
Other	
Other	
Other	
Other	
Other	
Other	
Other	
Other	
Other	
Other	
Other	
Other	
Other	

Notes

Notes

Notes

Notes

Part V
Basics of Estate Planning

This book is in no way meant to be a guide for understanding all there is to know about estate planning. That would, and does, require numerous volumes of books covering a wide array of topics and issues. While it is not my intention to explain the intricate nuances of estate planning strategies and procedures here, I do believe it is very important to give a brief overview of the subject, since it plays such a key role in the overall process that *Million Heirs* is designed to help you with. With that in mind, let's take a look at the basics.

Wills

One of the first things you need to be accustomed with is a will. A will is a declaration of how you wish your property be distributed. It could consist of one sentence, "I give everything I own to my wife" or more than 100 pages, as some wealthy individuals have discovered. It can be oral, handwritten, typed, or even e-mailed, but not all of these forms will be deemed legally binding or with sufficient reliability to be enforced. Additionally, some states give rights to your spouse or children that may give them the power to set aside or leave unenforced provisions in your validly executed will. With these requirements, you need to understand the process of making a will.

How Do I Make a Will?

Making a will can be a simple process. Many computer programs and self-help books are available to help someone make their own will. For more complicated planning, attorneys can provide assistance with proper drafting.

The first step in making a will is assessing what you own and who you want as beneficiary. Take a personal inventory of your assets. This book can help you create a personal financial statement. Be sure to consider all of your resources and beneficiaries. After you've determined what you own and whom you wish to benefit, the next step is constructing the plan. If you don't have a potential estate tax, then drafting your plan may only take a few sentences.

The final step is to make sure your will is properly formalized. An attorney can assist you with this step, or you may wish to complete this step alone as well. Generally, unless you live in a state that permits holographic wills, you should have your plan typed and witnessed by three witnesses (although some states permit two). The formalities surrounding the establishment of your will can make it desirable to seek the assistance of an attorney.

Do I Need an Attorney?

Because attorneys are often associated with conflict like litigation and divorce proceedings, the idea of consulting with an attorney scares some people. Many attorneys are like accountants or financial planners and seek to provide cost-effective solutions to drafting a will. Also, for complicated estates, attorneys can often provide solutions to complex decisions or remind you of potential problems with your plan that may prevent its challenge in court.

If any of the following factors apply to you, you should consider consulting an attorney:

- You wish to leave your spouse less than your entire estate
- You have a child that is not able to manage money well
- You have a physically handicapped child
- You have a mentally handicapped child
- You are the principal owner or manager of a business
- Your estate is greater than $500,000
- You have children from a former marriage
- You don't have anyone in mind for an executor
- You have children that are minors
- You wish to disinherit a child or spouse
- Your will is likely to be contested

As a general rule, if you have questions or doubts about your ability to draft your own will, it is safer and less expensive to seek professional help initially than to die with an invalid or incomplete estate planning document.

What Are Holographic Wills?

A holographic will is when you write your own will in your own handwriting. About twenty-five states allow handwritten wills, although it is rarely a good idea. A holographic will is usually not properly formalized (see next question) and may be incomplete. A holographic will may be better than nothing, but if you are taking the time to actually implement some estate planning, you should follow through and provide a complete plan. Be especially cautious about fill-in-the-blank wills or trusts. A fill-in-the-blank will that isn't properly formalized may be a holographic will that is only valid for those portions that you write in yourself. This could lead to unintended consequences or bequests. For example, there could be a blank line after the question, "Who do you wish to leave your personal items to?" You might write in "everything to my sister." Even if you contradict this information later in the document, it could be interpreted as giving everything to your sister, even your home and investment assets. This is the case even when this is obviously not what was intended.

Another problem with holographic wills is that in order to enforce their terms, the will must be proved in court, and that may involve formal hearings with handwriting experts that are extremely expensive, much more expensive than creating your will correctly initially. If you are going to take the time to establish a will, it only makes sense to be sure that the will is formalized.

How Do You Formalize a Will?

To be validly executed, a will must be written by an adult (usually over age eighteen), and the writer must be able to recognize his or her possessions and the persons or entities that they wish to benefit.

A validly executed will must meet several requirements to be considered formalized. The first requirement is that it be witnessed, usually by two or three witnesses. Most states require two, but in order to comply with all states, the use of three witnesses is highly recommended.

A witness must be independent. That means that each witness must have no interest in your will. They shouldn't be an executor, a beneficiary, or named in any way. Most witnesses must sign that they have witnessed your signature in their presence and that you appeared to be acting free from duress or pressure from anyone.

A second step may be to "prove" the will. Proving the will can be done after your death, but it is usually difficult or impossible to locate your witnesses at that time. Your will can be proved in advance by having your witnesses sign in the presence of a notary and attest under oath that you appeared to sign the will free from pressure or duress. This is obviously an additional step which may not be necessary. However, this may fall under the category of, "it's better to have it and not need it than to need it and not have it."

Additionally, the will should be dated, so that it can be determined which of two wills is your most recent, in the event that you have not destroyed a previously executed will. Wills do not need to be published or registered with anyone. Some states require a will to be dated. To determine the requirements in your state, seek assistance from an attorney.

How Do You Designate a Guardian for Children That Are Minors?

Another question which often arises is how to take care of minor children. Even if you don't have many assets to distribute, if you have children under the age of eighteen, a will can provide your recommendation for guardian in the event you and your spouse or partner both die in a common accident. Your advice is a recommendation only. Should the best interest of the child dictate otherwise, there is a chance that your recommendation will not be followed.

To increase the likelihood of your recommendation being followed, your will should be executed with all the formalities described above. Also, you and the child's other parent should both be consistent in your recommendation. If you absolutely cannot agree on a guardian (as is occasionally the case), one solution is to name both parties that you and your spouse wish to recommend and ask the judge to decide between those two. It is better to have the judge decide between two parties than to have the judge pick a third party that neither you nor the other parent wish to have raise your child.

The selection of a guardian is probably the most important decision in the will of a person with a child under the age of eighteen. You should talk over your decision with the guardian you name to make sure that they are willing to accept this incredible responsibility. At the same time, you should realize that absent a medical illness, the chance of your dying (or both you and your spouse dying) prior to your child turning eighteen is incredibly remote. More agony is raised from this decision than many others, and usually the matter is moot anyway.

In deciding who to name, there are relatively few requirements involved. This is more of a matter of preference. Your legal guardian should be an adult who you trust completely. You should probably consider close relatives and friends first. This is not a decision to be taken lightly. Spend time thinking about it before making this important decision.

How Do You Leave Property to Children?

Most states do not allow children to own property as an adult can. Since a child is deemed legally incapacitated, they are able to void contracts that they sign while a minor, although certain exceptions (like for necessities) are not voidable.

Because children can't transfer property without restrictions, you should not transfer any property of significant value to a child unless it is in trust or under your state's Uniform Transfers to Minors Act (UTMA) or Uniform Gifts to Minors Act (UGMA). You can avoid outright transfers by creating a trust in your will to hold property for your children until they attain a certain age.

You may wish to name a trustee that is different from the legal guardian that you name. For example, some people find that one relative is an excellent caregiver and would make a good guardian, while another relative is more financially savvy and will better protect their child's inheritance.

There are two basic forms of trusts for children. The first is a "pot" trust where all of your children's money is held and managed together. Think of a big pot of stew. You can require equal distributions or you can allow one or more children to be benefited at the expense of the other children. Sometimes this is desirable if certain facts may require more money for one child than another. For example, a child that has medical problems may require more care, attention, and money than another child.

Another common situation is educational trusts. If you have young children, you may want to allow for the possibility that one child will go to an expensive private school, while another child might go to a public school that is less expensive. You probably don't want to encourage your children to get a cheap education, so a pot trust might encourage the maximum quality of education. Using the stew analogy, one child may be hungrier than another, and you can give your trustee discretion to decide how to distribute the pot of money.

For situations not requiring special care, it may be better to separate each child's trust. This allows each child to contribute to investment decisions if you desire, and doesn't reward those children who spend more than others at the expense of their sibling(s). You can name different trustees for each child and depending upon the child's age and maturity level, you may want to name them as a co-trustee. This is probably more advisable in the situation where the child's share is still in trust, even though they may be twenty-five or thirty.

Can I Disinherit My Children or Spouse?

This is a complicated question and should be directed to an attorney familiar with the laws of your state. Most states require some protection for the spouse in the form of an elective share. A spouse who elects against the will forfeits the recovery under the will in exchange for a statutory formula. Generally, it is some percentage of your estate. The modern uniform probate code (adopted in a few states, but potentially adoptable by all states) requires a sliding scale formula for your spouse based upon the number of years of marriage.

Children generally may be disinherited, but it must be obvious that it is your intention. Most states have "pretermitted heir" statutes that require that children not named in your will be given a share as if you had no will. This is to protect children that you may have after the creation of your will. It is assumed that you would want a child included. Thus, if you wish to intentionally omit a child, it is better to explicitly state that intention in your will.

What Happens If My Will is Challenged?

Most wills are not challenged. Only a handful are ever disputed in court, and the success ratio of challenged wills is generally quite small. A challenge may be brought by an heir who asserts that your will was not executed properly (see above), unintentionally omitted them (generally only children or spouses), or was fraudulently executed.

An example of a fraudulently executed will is when another heir uses their position or authority to require someone to execute a will that they would not otherwise sign. This is usually referred to as undue duress and can occur if a caretaker or other fiduciary is given an interest in an estate that is not consistent with the normal wishes of an individual.

What is a Power of Attorney?

A power of attorney is a document that allows someone to manage your affairs on your behalf, while you are still living. A power of attorney can be effective for someone who is incapacitated or for someone who is extremely healthy for the sake of convenience.

Basically, a power of attorney appoints a power holder, often referred to as an "attorney-in-fact" to sign or execute documents as though you signed them yourself. If you give authority to someone to act on your behalf and they act contrary to your wishes, you may be responsible for that action, although you may have a recovery right against your power holder.

If a power of attorney is "durable," then it will survive your incapacity. A nondurable power of attorney is no longer effective once you become legally incapacitated. Generally, a power of attorney is intended to be durable, because that is precisely the situation it is intended to cover. Sometimes, however, a power of attorney is limited to a specific purpose. For example, if you were purchasing a home and were unable to attend the closing, you might grant your spouse a limited power of attorney for the sole purpose of signing the closing papers associated with the loan.

What is the Effective Date of a Power of Attorney?

A power of attorney is effective when you state that it is. The example at the end of this section provides that the power is effective when you sign the document. A power of attorney can go into effect at a later date or upon your legal incapacity. This power of attorney is often called a springing power, because it springs into existence at a date in the future.

What Are The Powers That You Can Grant to Your Attorney-in-fact?

You can generally give your attorney-in-fact most or all financial rights that you have. For example, you can provide that your attorney-in-fact can act in the following ways:

- Pay bills as they become due
- File your income tax return for federal or state purposes
- Collect your Social Security or Veterans benefits
- Invest your funds in stocks, bonds, or other assets
- Borrow money on your behalf
- Write checks as necessary
- Manage your business
- Represent you in court as a defendant
- Make distributions from your 401(k) or pension fund
- Sue someone on your behalf

You cannot generally give your power holder certain powers that are perceived as personal and nonassignable. For example, your attorney-in-fact cannot normally do the following on your behalf:

- Create or modify your will
- Revise your testamentary disposition
- Marry or divorce
- Make medical treatment decisions

Why Should I Have a Power of Attorney?

A power of attorney makes a great deal of sense when you consider the alternative, not having a power of attorney. If you become incapacitated without a power of attorney, it is too late to create a power of attorney.

If you become incapacitated without a durable power of attorney, your heirs will be forced to seek a formal guardianship to manage your affairs. This is an expensive legal process and requires testimony on your capacity and usually at least one hearing before a judge. Your entire family must be notified and consent or challenge the appointment. If you have children with differing viewpoints on who should be your guardian, the expense of a formal guardianship can exceed $10,000 very quickly.

Even after the appointment, the court must maintain jurisdiction and oversee your affairs. Your guardian will be required to file annual accountings and inventories to show that your funds are being spent for your care. Additionally, your guardian may need court approval to sell your assets.

Another problem is that your formal guardian may be required to post bond, which can be rather expensive. Similar to the bond posted by a criminal, your guardian is posting bond to insure that your funds will not be stolen. The cost of the bond can be as high as one or two percent of your assets, depending upon the length of time the bond is needed.

On the other hand, a power of attorney can be created as easily as filling out the form attached at the end of this section. You must check to see if your state has a different form. Some states have a specialized form different from the attached form. If properly executed and notarized, you can create the power of attorney for the cost of this book (and maybe a few dollars for a notary). If you are very likely to need to use a power of attorney, you should consider requesting a form from your attorney.

How Long Can a Power of Attorney Last?

The power of attorney can last only until your death. Many heirs who have been managing a relative's finances under a power of attorney mistakenly think that they can continue to write checks and act on their behalf after they die. However, a durable power cannot extend past death. At death, your executor becomes your attorney-in-fact, once they are formally appointed.

An important distinction in the amount of time which the power of attorney will last is the type of power it is. If your power of attorney is not durable, it will end upon your incapacity. Incapacity is the point at which you are no longer able to make decisions on your own behalf and its legal definition varies from state to state. Generally, if a doctor states that you need assistance, you may be deemed legally incapacitated. It is more difficult in some situations. For example, an Alzheimer's patient may at times be incapacitated and at other times be completely sane. For safety, if Alzheimer's is in your family you should consider creating a non-springing power of attorney. This will make sure that you are always protected in the event of temporary spells of incapacity.

My Financial Broker Won't Recognize the Attached Form, Why Not?

Financial institutions including banks and brokers often require that you execute a special power of attorney that they have specifically prepared. There is no legal basis for their failure to recognize your power of attorney. This is purely a matter of preference.

Usually, they will require special powers of attorney for expedience. If everyone's power of attorney at Charles Schwab or Merrill Lynch (for example) looks the same, there is no question about its validity. If you can execute a form with each financial institution before your incapacity you should do so. Problems avoided equals money saved. However, if you are attempting to use a power and the person granting the power is incapacitated, you should seek advice from an attorney to implement the power.

Description of Attached Form

The attached power of attorney is extremely broad. It is designed for someone that you trust explicitly like your spouse or a child. It is effective upon signing and can be given to the power holder immediately.

A provision is made for a successor power of attorney, in the event of the death or incapacity of the first power holder. Failing to keep your estate planning documents current can mean that you appoint a power holder who is already dead or incapacitated.

This document is merely a form, and you should check your state regulations or check with an attorney to ensure that it will work in your state.

What is Probate?

Since you cannot take your property with you to your next life, a process called probate exists to provide for the smooth transition of wealth from one generation to the next. Probate has a very negative image, but is not in itself bad. Most of the problems occur due to the amount of time involved in the probate process.

The best way to illustrate exactly what the probate process is all about is by breaking it down and looking at its various components. Probate is the name of the legal process that involves:

1. Proving that your will is, in fact, your will
2. Providing notice to the relevant people that a person has died
3. Creating an inventory of a person's assets
4. Valuing assets for tax purposes, including appraisals and valuations
5. Paying all valid debts, including final income and estate taxes
6. Distributing property as dictated by a will.

Although only a few major steps are involved, the importance of a thorough and complete probate cannot be underestimated. For example, if step #2 is not properly met, then a person can sue a decedent many months or years after their death. This can create a whole new set of problems.

Probate fees are paid from your estate and involve creating paperwork and meeting legal formalities. The expense of probate can be very minimal in a small estate or extremely expensive for a large estate with a protracted probate proceeding. Probate may be desired if your estate consists largely of debts or assets that are not subject to easy valuation. But keep in mind that there can be a lot of work involved which can mean a lot of fees involved.

How Long Does the Probate Process Typically Take?

The length of probate depends upon the assets of the estate and certain factors of state law. It can take many years in some circumstances or a few weeks in others. Normally, probate takes about a year and a half.

Who is in Charge of Probate?

A will usually names an executor who is the overseer of the probate process. He or she is responsible for making sure the steps are met. The executor usually will hire an attorney and an accountant for assistance, but that is not necessary in all estates.

To select your executor, you should pick someone who you trust with your finances. There are some legal checks and balances, but a dishonest executor can often cheat your heirs or other beneficiaries. Usually, the primary beneficiary of your estate is a good start, unless certain circumstances dictate otherwise (like incapacity).

Sometimes an executor is not needed. For example, if you own only a few assets, many states will let you dispense with administration or probate your will by short form to avoid an expensive proceeding. Also, if your estate only consists of joint assets then there is no estate to probate. If there are only a few assets in your name, your relative may simply agree to distribute the assets as you desired and forego probate. They can decide among themselves how to best accomplish this goal.

If there is a possibility for disagreement, it is best to go through the formalities of probate to ensure that no one is cheated or disadvantaged.

Who Would be a Good Executor?

The process of executing a will requires someone that is good with details and attentive. It can be a tedious process, but it doesn't necessarily entail legal or accounting expertise. Something to be aware of is that all of your legal questions can be answered by a competent attorney. Remember, though, that the expense of attorneys and accountants will be borne by your estate. Honesty and common sense are more valuable than financial acumen.

The executor's main goal is to protect the estate from invalid claims and to pay valid claims. They are required to distribute the assets as the will dictates.

Now that we've reviewed some of the basics of estate planning, it is important that you understand the significance of implementing some of these strategies into your own plan. Leaving behind a well thought-out plan for how your estate will be handled and/or distributed can be one of the most thoughtful things which you can do for your heirs. The key is to actually do it.

DURABLE POWER OF ATTORNEY

KNOW ALL MEN BY THESE PRESENTS:

That I, ______________________________ of (City)________________, (County)________________, (State)______________, do hereby constitute and appoint ________________________, of (City)________________, (State)______________, my attorney-in-fact to manage and conduct all of my property and affairs and for that purpose and in my name to do any act or execute any instrument pertaining to any of my real or personal property, business and affairs, as fully and to all intents and purposes as I might or could do if personally present and acting on my own behalf. This Power of Attorney shall not be affected by my subsequent disability or incapacity.

Without limiting or in any manner restricting the foregoing, I further and specifically authorize ____________________________ as my attorney-in-fact:

1. To deposit and withdraw, in my name, in and from any banking, brokerage or other financial institution, any funds which may come into my hands or into my attorney's hands on my behalf.
2. To receive, receipt for, endorse, make, sign, execute, acknowledge and deliver any checks, notes, deeds, agreements, certificates, receipts or any other instruments in writing of whatsoever kind and nature concerning any of my real or personal property, business, or affairs including, without limiting the foregoing, the endorsements of checks payable to me individually or jointly with others, the changing of the beneficiary or beneficiaries of any insurance policy or policies which I may own and the filing of claims on any hospitalization, sickness, or disability insurance which I may own.
3. To sell, transfer, assign, pledge or surrender any stocks, bonds, or certificates of ownership or indebtedness which I may own and which may presently or hereafter be issued to me individually or as a co-owner with others.
4. To buy, sell, convey, transfer, assign, mortgage, pledge or otherwise encumber or dispose of any personal property or real property which I may presently or hereafter own either individually or jointly with others.
5. To take, hold, possess, invest, lease, and otherwise manage any and all of my property or any interest therein; to eject, remove, or relieve tenants or other persons from, and recover possession of, such property by all lawful means; and to maintain, protect, preserve, insure, remove, store, transport, repair, rebuild, modify, or improve the same or any part thereof.
6. To make, do, and transact all and every kind of business of whatsoever nature or kind, including the receipt, recovery, collection, payment, compromise, settlement,

and adjustment of all accounts, legacies, bequests, interests, dividends, annuities, demands, debts, taxes, and obligations, which may now or hereafter be due or payable by me or to me.

7. To institute, prosecute, defend, compromise, arbitrate, and otherwise conduct any legal or equitable actions, suits, litigation, or proceedings in connection with any of my property or affairs.
8. To act as my attorney or proxy with respect to any stocks, shares, bonds or other investments, rights, or interests that I may now or hereafter hold.
9. To engage and dismiss agents, counsel, and employees in connection with the management, protection, disposal, or conduct of any of my property or business affairs.
10. To prepare, execute, and file federal, state, or other jurisdictions' income, gift, property, and other tax returns, claims, governmental reports, applications, requests, and documents.
11. To open, establish, remove any items from, or add any items to any safe-deposit box or other similar repository.
12. To open, terminate, direct, and otherwise exercise control over any brokerage account with any brokerage house, investment banking firm, trust company, bank, or other financial institution.
13. To make gifts on my behalf to my wife/husband, my children, and their descendants, either outright or in trust, for purposes which the agent deems to be in my best interest, specifically including minimizing income, estate, inheritance, or gift taxes (but no attorney-in-fact hereunder may make gifts to himself or herself during the calendar year in excess of the amount specified in Internal Revenue Code section 2503(b), as amended from time to time).

My attorney-in-fact may not amend any Trust established by me nor make or modify my will.

Subject to the limitations stated above, it is my intention in executing this instrument, to delegate to ______________________________________, as my agent and attorney-in-fact, with full power to substitute one or more attorneys, full, absolute, and complete power and authority to represent me in all matters concerning me, my affairs, my business, and my real and personal property as fully as I might do and as if I had done if personally acting in my own behalf, and I hereby ratify and confirm each and every thing whatsoever my said attorney may do in my name or on my behalf.

If ______________________________________ should be or become unable or unwilling to serve as my attorney-in-fact hereunder, then I appoint ______________________________________ as his/her substitute with all the powers granted hereunder.

IN WITNESS WHEREOF, I have hereunto set my hand this _______ day of ______, _____.

____

____

ACKNOWLEDGMENT

STATE OF (STATE))
) SS.
COUNTY OF (COUNTY))

Before me, the undersigned duly commissioned, qualified and acting Notary Public within and for the County and State aforesaid, personally appeared, to me well known, and stated that he/she signed and acknowledged the foregoing Durable Power of Attorney as his/her voluntary act and deed.

WITNESS my hand and seal this __________ day of __________, _____.

____

Notary Public

My Commission Expires:

____

Will

Do you have a will? _____ Yes _____ No

If yes, please answer the following questions.

Where is your will stored? ______________________________

____

What type of will? ______________________________

____

Who is the executor? ______________________________

____

Who drafted your will? ______________________________

____

Who are the guardians of any minor children? ______________________________

____

Who are the trustees of any trust created in your will? ______________________________

____

Do you have durable power of attorney? ______________________________

____

Basics of Estate Planning

Estate Planner

Do you have an estate planner or estate planning attorney? _____ Yes _____ No

If yes, please answer the following questions.

Who is your estate planner (name and phone number)? ________________________________

____

Where is a copy of your estate plan? ________________________________

____

Revocable Trust

Do you have a revocable trust? _____ Yes _____ No

If yes, please answer the following question.

Where is your revocable trust located? ________________________________

Notes

Notes

Notes

Notes

Notes

Part VI
Medical Information

Some of the most important information which must be provided to your heirs upon your death is that relating to your medical condition. Special medical conditions are extremely important in times of crisis. By fully documenting any special conditions in advance, problems can be avoided in the event you are unconscious or unable to provide specific information or instructions.

The number and type of documents needed is also an item which should be documented. One of the most important documents will be the living will. Because of its importance, you need to understand exactly what it is. A living will is a vital part of any estate plan. It provides that upon certain conditions, a physician may remove various instruments of life support or fail to provide certain treatments that would prolong a condition that is unlikely to improve.

Another important document to be included in your medical information section is a healthcare directive. A healthcare directive appoints an individual as a person who can make treatment decisions concerning you. Because this item is so important, a sample healthcare directive document, as well as accompanying documents, is included in this section.

Always remember that the more information you keep, the better it will be for your family. The problem, however, is that this information needs to be kept in an orderly manner. Far too often, individuals will mistakenly believe that they have done a great job in saving their important documents but they leave behind a mountain of paper for their heirs to sift through. While these people feel that they've done a great job, they have actually made matters worse by leaving their families in a situation which seems overwhelming.

The key is to maintain documents in a simple, straightforward manner which can enable your family to operate much more smoothly. By answering the questions posed in this section, you can be well on your way to making things much easier for yourself during your lifetime and for your heirs upon your death.

Living Will

Do you have a living will? _____ Yes _____ No

If yes, please answer the following question.

Where is your living will located? ______________________________

____

Medical Information

Who is your personal physician? ______________________________

Who is your primary insurance with? ______________________________

Do you receive Medicare or Medicaid benefits? ______________________________

Do you have a hospital preference? ______________________________

Any allergies to medicines? ______________________________

Any special conditions that a doctor should be aware of? ______________________________

Do you have a health-care proxy? ______________________________

Do you wish to be an organ donor? ______________________________

Notes

Notes

Part VII
Tax and Benefits Reference Materials

e've all heard the saying, "only two things in life are guaranteed: death and taxes." While this statement is generally correct, in the year of death it is not the deceased who has to worry about filing that next tax return. What was once a fairly simple process can become a tremendous burden for the ones you leave behind.

In this section, we discuss questions such as: how do I file?, how do I report income?, how do I sign the return?, and how do I claim a refund? While this section addresses only the basic principles in filing your taxes in the year of death, IRS Publication 559 has been included as an appendix to this book. This publication gives specific details on how to handle the different situations that might arise. This information can become extremely complex. Please consult your tax advisor for further information on filing an income tax return for a decedent.

Filing Status

If one spouse dies during the current tax year, the surviving spouse can file jointly if they meet the requirements to file jointly on the date of death and the surviving spouse did not remarry during the year. Taxpayers are entitled to file a joint return if, on the date of death:

- Taxpayers were married and living together
- Taxpayers were married and living apart, but not legally separated under a decree of divorce
- Living in a common-law marriage, recognized by the state

In the tax year immediately following the year of death, the surviving spouse would file single unless he or she had remarried. If the surviving spouse maintained his or her home for the entire year as the main house for his or her child, stepchild, adopted child, or foster child, the surviving taxpayer might be eligible for qualifying widow or widower status. This status allows the surviving spouse to use the same tax rates as married filing jointly for two years after the year of death. To qualify for this tax status, the taxpayer must:

- Maintain a home as the main home for his or her child, step child, adopted child, or foster child for the entire year
- Provide more than 50 percent of the cost of maintaining the household
- The child, stepchild, adopted child, or foster child above qualifies as the taxpayer's dependent
- Taxpayer was eligible to file jointly for the tax year in which his or her spouse died
- Taxpayer did not remarry as of the end of the current tax year

To better understand how this works, let's take a look at an example. Assume Bob and Sue were married and had two children, Jack and Jill. Bob passed away on November 11, 1998. Sue meets all of the qualifications mentioned above. For the 1998 tax year, Sue would file a joint return with Bob as surviving spouse. For the 1999 and 2000 tax year, Sue would file as qualifying widow. For the 2001 tax year, Sue would file as head of household.

Assume the same facts above except that Bob and Sue had no children. For the 1998 tax year, Sue would file a joint return with Bob as surviving spouse. For the 1999 tax year, Sue would file single.

Filling Out the Tax Form

The word "deceased," the decedent's name, and the date of death should be written across the top of the tax return. If filing a joint return, fill in the decedent and surviving spouse's name, address, and Social Security number where requested on IRS Form 1040. If a joint return is not being filed, the decedent's name should be written in the name space in care of the personal representative. The personal representative's name and address should be written in the remaining spaces.

If a personal representative has been appointed, he or she must sign the return. If the return is a joint return, the surviving spouse must also sign the return. If no personal representative has been appointed, the surviving spouse should sign the return and write "filing as surviving spouse" in the signature area. If there is no personal representative or surviving spouse, the person in charge of the decedent's property must sign the return as personal representative.

How to Report Income

If the decedent was a cash method taxpayer, income received before death must be separated from income received after death. If the decedent was an accrual taxpayer, income earned or accrued before death must be separated from income earned or accrued after death. Income before death is taxed to the decedent on his or her personal tax return (single, joint, separate, head of household). Income after death, also referred to as income in respect of the decedent, is taxed to the estate or the beneficiary who received the income.

It is not uncommon for W-2s or 1099 interest and dividend forms to be reported incorrectly to the taxpayer in the year of death. If possible, an attempt should be made to obtain a correct reporting form from the issuing organization. An employer can reissue a W-2 form. If a corrected 1099 INT or 1099 DIV cannot be obtained, report the total interest or dividend reported on these forms on Schedule B of Form 1040. Subtotal these amounts along with interest and dividends reported from other sources. Subtract any interest or dividends belonging to another recipient, in this case interest or dividends that should be reported to the estate or to the beneficiary who received the income. Identify this adjustment as "nominee distribution." Forms 1096, 1099 INT, and Form 1099 DIV must be filed with the IRS. Also, Forms 1099-INT and 1099-DIV should be sent to the estate or to the beneficiary who received the income.

How to Report S Corporation Income, Deductions, or Losses

The decedent's pro rata share of S Corporation income or loss up to the date of death is reported on the decedent's final tax return. The decedent's pro rata share of S Corporation income or loss after death is reported on the tax return of the estate for the individual who has acquired the decedent's stock in the S Corporation.

How to Report Partnership Income and Loss

Partnership income is generally taxed in two ways: income tax and self-employment tax. Each of these specific types of tax are treated differently for a decedent.

First, let's take a look at partnership income. Do not include the distributive share of partnership income for a partnership's tax year ending after the decedent's death on the final return of the decedent. Partnership income earned up to and including the date of death is income in respect of the decedent and is reported to the estate or the successor in the partnership interest. To better understand this, consider the following example.

Max is a partner in a calendar year partnership, meaning the tax year ends December 31, 1998. Max died on October 15, 1998. Partnership income or loss for the tax year 1998 is not reported on Max's final tax return. The entire amount of partnership income or loss for the tax year 1998 is reported to the estate or the successor in the partnership interest.

Now, let's take a look at self-employment income. For self-employment tax purposes, self-employment income for the decedent includes the decedent's distributive share of a partnership's income or loss through the end of the month in which death occurred. This can be explained better through the use of an example.

Assume Heather is a partner in a partnership which has a fiscal year-end of June 30, 1998. However, Heather is a calendar year taxpayer. Heather died on December 10, 1998. Heather's interest in the partnership is assigned to her brother, Barry. The partnership reported income of $50,000 for the tax year ending June 30, 1998. Of that $50,000, Heather's share was $10,000.

The partnership reported income of $75,000 for the tax year ending June 30, 1999. Of this amount, Heather's distributive share was $15,000. Income is determined to be distributed evenly throughout the year. The tax implications for the above scenario are as follows:

- Heather reports her share of income ($10,000) for the partnership tax year ending June 30, 1998, on her final return because the partnership tax year ended before Heather's death.
- Heather reports self-employment income of $10,000 for the partnership tax year ending June 30, 1998, on her final return.
- Barry reports the share of income ($15,000) for the partnership tax year ending June 30, 1999, on his personal 1999 tax return because the partnership tax year ended after Heather's death.
- Heather also reports self-employment income of $7,500 on her final tax return for the partnership tax year ending June 30, 1999. This represents $^{6}/_{12}$ of this self-employment income for the partnership year ending June 30, 1999. This is due to the fact that she was alive during six of the 12 months of that tax year.
- Barry reports the remaining $7,500 as self-employment income on his personal 1999 tax return. This is due to the fact that Heather passed away midway through the partnership's tax year.

How to Claim a Refund

If a joint return is filed with a surviving spouse and there is no appointed estate representative, no additional supporting material is needed to claim a refund. If a court appointed or certified personal representative is filing for the deceased taxpayer, a copy of the court certificate showing the representative's authority and capacity to file the return must be attached to the return. Any other person who is filing a return for a decedent and claiming a refund must file Form 1310, Statement of Person Claiming Refund Due a Deceased Taxpayer, with the return. A sample copy of this form is included on page 136 of this book.

Life Insurance Death Proceeds

The proceeds from a decedent's life insurance policy paid by reason of death are generally excluded from income. This exclusion is not limited to the deceased's immediate family. It applies to any beneficiary. If insurance proceeds are to be received in installments, the proceeds must be allocated between insurance proceeds and interest income. The interest portion of such an agreement would be reported as income on Form 1040, Schedule B or on Form 1040A, Schedule 1.

Basis of Inherited Property

It is important to note that your basis for property that you inherit changes. Your basis is an important number because it will be the basis for which future taxable gains or losses will be computed. Basis for property inherited is generally one of the following:

- The fair market value of the property at the date of death
- The fair market value on the alternate valuation date if elected by the personal representative of the estate
- Special use valuation for real property used in farming or an other closely held business

While this explanation of basis is general in nature, it is important to understand that basis in property can change at the date of death.

It is common for elderly people to have owned their homes for many years. In today's real estate environment, the price your parents paid to buy their current home is probably substantially less than what they could sell it for today. This would be true with just about any piece of real property. If that property were inherited by you, you would get to "step-up" your basis in that property to its current fair market value. This could provide valuable income tax savings to you in the future. If you inherited your parent's home, you would either: sell, rent out, use as your main home, or use it as a second home. In all of these situations, a higher tax basis could mean future income tax savings whether as basis for property sold or through depreciation.

As a rule of thumb, when property is inherited, it is imperative that it be appraised. This will save you time and trouble in the future. This is not meant to be a complete discussion on basis in inherited property. Please consult with your tax advisor for more detailed information on this topic.

As mentioned earlier, IRS Publication 559, Survivors, Executors, and Administrators, has been included in this book. Please refer to this publication and to your tax advisor for more detailed information the topics discussed in this section.

Income taxes are not simple in a normal year, much less in a year in which a death occurs. Income tax laws are constantly changing. Rules and laws in place now might not be the same laws you will have to deal with in the future. Keep yourself abreast of current income and estate tax law changes. The IRS phone number for ordering forms and general information is 1-800-TAX-FORM (1-800-829-3676).

Many small businesses operate without the full-time assistance of a bookkeeper, accountant, or CPA. These professionals, if utilized at all, usually assist small businesses during tax season. Income taxes, however, are only a small percentage of the total taxes a business may be required to file and pay.

The relating forms, taxes, and due dates can be a nearly impossible task for a surviving spouse to decipher. While it would be recommended to engage the services of a professional, some will attempt to carry on business operations without incurring any additional expense.

The following information represents basic summaries of small businesses and the related taxes and forms they might be required to pay and file. These summaries are not intended to be an all-inclusive guide to operating a small business. They merely represent the basic tax and reporting requirements of small businesses. Please consult your tax advisor for further information regarding these topics.

Small Business Entities - Basic Tax Implications

I. Sole Proprietorship
   1. Report profit/loss on IRS Form 1040 Schedule C due April 15.
   2. Schedule C net loss can be used to offset other (W-2) income.
   3. Schedule C profit taxed two ways:
      A. Income tax is paid on Schedule C net profit at the taxpayers individual rate.
      B. Self-employment tax is paid on Schedule C profit at 15.3%.
   4. Profit must be shown in three out of five years or IRS could make you prove the activity is a "for profit business."

II. Partnership
   1. Report partnership Profit/Loss on Form 1065 due April 15.
   2. Partnership itself pays no income tax.
   3. Individual partner's share of profit/loss is allocated on Form 1065 Schedule K-1.
   4. Profit/Loss from Schedule K-1 flows to the individual taxpayer on Schedule E, page 2.
   5. Partner's share of loss can be used to offset other individual (W-2) income.
   6. Partner's share of profit is taxed in two ways:
      A. Income tax is paid at the taxpayer's individual rates.

B. Self-employment tax is paid on partnership profits, whether withdrawn or not, at 15.3%.

III. S Corporation

1. Report S Corporation Profit/Loss on Form 1120 S due March 15.
2. S Corporation itself generally pays no tax.
3. Shareholder's portion of profit/loss is allocated on Form 1120 S, Schedule K-1.
4. Profit/Loss from Schedule K-1 flows to the individual taxpayer on Schedule E, page 2.
5. Officers of the corporation must be paid "reasonable wage" for services performed.
6. Shareholder's portion of loss can be used to offset other (W-2) income if the loss is not greater than the shareholder's at risk basis.
7. S Corporation net income is taxed at the shareholder's individual tax rate in addition to the amount taken by the shareholder as salary.
8. S Corporation net income not taken out as salary is generally not subject to self-employment tax.

IV. C Corporation

1. Report C Corporation Profit/Loss on Form 1120 due on the 15th day of the third month following the close of the tax year.
2. C Corporation is recognized by the IRS as a separate taxpaying entity.
3. C Corporation can file a six month extension on Form 7004.
4. C Corporations distribute profits to its shareholders through dividends.
5. Dividends are taxable to the recipient, but not a deduction for the Corporation.

V. Limited Liability Company (LLC)

1. Created and regulated under state law.
2. Can be taxed as a partnership, corporation, or in some states, a sole proprietorship.
3. Generally, LLCs are taxed as partnerships.
4. Owners are referred to as members rather than partners or shareholders.

Small Business Entities - Basic Business Taxes

I. Business Taxes

1. Federal Tax Deposit (withholding, Social Security, Medicare) due on the 15th of the month (unless required by IRS to pay semimonthly).
2. State withholding - varies by state.
3. State sales and use tax - varies by state.
4. Federal Unemployment - due quarterly.
5. State Unemployment - varies by state.
6. Corporate estimates (C Corporation only) due quarterly.

II. Personal Taxes

1. Personal tax estimates (sole proprietorship, partnership, S Corporation)

Due: April 15th
June 15th
September 15th
January 15th

III. Tax Forms
1. Quarterly
    A. Federal Form 941
2. Annually
    A. Federal Form 940 (Federal Unemployment)
    B. W-2s
    C. 1099s
    D. Federal Form W-3
    E. State Withholding

IV. Additional Forms and Filings
1. Local Business License
2. Fictitious Name statement
3. Franchise tax
4. Real Estate tax
5. Personal Property tax
6. State Unemployment tax (due date varies by state)
7. State Withholding (due date varies by state)

Insurance

In today's world of planning an estate, the power of a life insurance policy cannot be overlooked. Life insurance policies can be used to increase the value of your estate, provide financial security to your beneficiaries, accumulate a cash surrender value, and provide income at retirement, as well as numerous other functions.

Many large estates are made up mainly of real property and business interests with a relatively small amount of liquid assets. This can prove to be a huge potential problem to heirs. For example, let's say your parents left you and your brother the following estate:

House	$250,000
Business interests	$500,000
Cash	$200,000
Investments	$50,000
Retirement Plans	$300,000
Building	$700,000
Life Insurance	$0

The total value of the estate would be $2 million, which will generate estate taxes in the neighborhood of $400,000 to $450,000. In this example, your parents only had $200,000 in cash. In order to pay the estate taxes, you and your brother would have to sell the house, business interests, investments, or building, which could trigger potential additional taxes. You could also take out a loan against the real property and incur additional costs and interest. All of this could have been avoided with the proper planning and insurance policy. Please consult your insurance advisor for the insurance policy that best fits your needs.

Locating a specific insurance policy at death can be very difficult. In the case of a missing or lost insurance policy, the policy can be located by contacting:

Missing Policy Search
American Council of Life Insurance
1001 Pennsylvania Avenue N.W.
Washington, D.C. 20004

In the next few paragraphs, we will look at some different types of life insurance products and the key differences between them. Regardless of the financial objective, there is an insurance policy that meets your needs.

Term Insurance

Term Insurance provides financial protection for a specific period of time for a specified dollar amount. Fixed premium payments are due for the term of the policy. If you live past the term of the policy, the policy and the financial protection expires. The holder of the policy is usually given the option to renew at a higher premium.

Advantages:

- Cheaper than other forms of life insurance
- Can be renewed at end of term
- Can be converted to permanent insurance at end of term
- Immediate protection

Disadvantages:

- Expires at end of term if not renewed
- Premiums increase with each renewal
- Policies generally cut off around age 65
- No cash surrender value is accumulated
- Purchasing only death benefit

Whole Life Insurance

Whole Life Insurance provides financial protection at a constant premium. It will pay off whenever the insured dies, rather than within a specified term. The premiums are broken into two categories: insurance protection and investment. As you grow older, the cash value of your policy rises. This allows the insurance or risk protection to drop allocating a larger portion of your premiums to investments.

Advantages:

- Financial protection for life of insured
- Accumulates cash value tax free
- Builds a cash value available for borrowing

Disadvantages:

- More expensive than term insurance
- Rate of return on investment is not guaranteed
- Premiums in the early years go mainly towards costs of the policy, not investments

Variable Life Insurance

This type of policy is similar to a Whole Life policy. Variable Life Insurance provides financial protection at a constant premium. It provides a cash value and a guaranteed minimum death benefit. The primary difference is the insured can elect his or her cash value be invested in stock, bonds, money market funds, real estate securities, et cetera. If the cash value of the investments has exceeded the policy's assumed rate of growth, the excess will be added to the face value of the policy. The face value of the policy will be distributed to your beneficiaries tax free upon your death.

Advantages:

- Investment in potential growth of equities
- Guaranteed minimum death benefit
- Accumulates tax free
- Excess earnings added to amount of policy

Disadvantages:

- More expensive than other types of insurance
- Cash value fluctuates with investment performance
- Death benefit fluctuates with investment performance

Universal Life Insurance

Universal Life provides Term Life protection with an investment program. Once the initial premium is paid, annual fixed premiums are no longer required. Monthly premiums can even be paid out of the cash value as long as it maintains a sufficient cash balance to meet the premium. Interest is earned tax free at current market rates.

Advantages:

- Interest is earned tax free
- Insurance protection for life of insured
- Builds a cash value available for borrowing

Disadvantages:

- Not a good savings tool

When purchasing a life insurance policy, be certain you understand exactly what insurance and investment options you are buying. Consult with competent advisors. Not all insurance agents have your best interests in mind. Also, read over the insurance policy after you have purchased it. A purchaser of an insurance policy has ten days to cancel it and receive a full refund after he or she receives it in the mail.

Health Insurance

COBRA (Consolidated Omnibus Budget Reconciliation Act) is a federal law which allows a surviving spouse and dependent children to continue their health coverage under the insured's plan at work for a limited period of time. This coverage is provided for a minimum of 36 months. The survivor's premium generally cannot exceed the current cost of coverage plus an additional 2% to cover the employer's administrative costs.

Social Security Benefits For Survivors

Social Security is generally thought of as a government enforced retirement plan. Not only does Social Security offer retirement benefits for the retired taxpayer, benefits for the taxpayer's spouse and children might also be available. In addition to these benefits, Social Security also provides disability benefits and survivor benefits.

This section will focus on survivor benefits. This is probably the least known facet of the Social Security program. Widow(er)s, children, dependent parents, and even former spouses could qualify for survivor benefits. This section will briefly discuss how you qualify for benefits, who is eligible for benefits, and what the benefits are. Please consult your tax advisor, attorney, or financial planner for further information on Social Security benefits.

To provide benefits for your heirs you must have accumulated enough credits while you were working. Credits are accumulated by earning wages (either as an employee or self employed). In 1998, Social Security taxpayers earn one credit for every $700 earned. For every year you work you are eligible to earn up to four credits. Therefore, if a taxpayer earns $2,800 in 1998, he or she has earned four credits. The amount of earnings needed to obtain one credit is adjusted each year for inflation. Credits do not depend on the amount of money you make over the maximum credit wage base. A person who makes $20,000 a year earns the same amount of credits as a person who makes $600,000 a year.

The taxpayer's age determines the number of credits needed to be fully qualified. To compute the number of credits needed to fully qualify, take the year before their death and subtract the year they turned 21. For example, if they turned 21 in 1972 and died in 1995 then they would need 22 credits to be fully qualified (1994-1972).

If a taxpayer does not qualify for survivor benefits under the above qualifications, Social Security benefits can be paid to the deceased taxpayer's spouse and children. To qualify, the deceased taxpayer would need to have earned at least six credits in the three years preceding his or her death.

Widows and Widowers

- Must be age 60 or older
- Must be age 50 or older if disabled
- Can be any age if taking care of worker's child(ren) under age sixteen
- Can be any age if taking care of worker's disabled child who is receiving Social Security benefits

Children

- Must not be married
- Must be under age 18
- Must be under age 19 if a full-time high school student
- Any age and disabled if disability occurred before age 22

Parents

- Must qualify as dependent of worker
- Must be age 62 or older

Former Spouse

- Must be age 60 or older
- Must be age 50 or older if disabled
- Must have been married to worker for at least 10 years

- Any age and caring for workers children under age 16 or disabled and receiving Social Security benefits (no length of marriage provision)
- Must be unmarried unless remarriage occurred after age 60
- Must be unmarried unless disabled and remarriage occurred after age 50

Death Benefit

If the deceased taxpayer had accumulated enough credits to provide Social Security survivor benefits for his family, a one-time death benefit of $255 is paid to his or her spouse or minor children.

Widows and Widowers

- 100% of worker's benefit at full retirement age
- Percentage decreases if widow(er) draws benefits before full age of retirement
- 75% of worker's benefit if caring for child who is under 16 or disabled and receiving Social Security benefits

Children

- 75% of worker's benefit

Parents

- 75% of worker's benefit for each parent
- 82.5% of worker's benefit for only one parent

Former Spouse

- 100% of worker's benefit at full retirement age
- Percentage decreases if widow(er) draws benefits before full age or retire ment
- 75% of worker's benefit if caring for child who is under 16 or disabled and receiving Social Security benefits

If you are an heir who is eligible for Social Security survivor benefits, you should apply immediately. You will need to supply a copy of the insured person's death certificate and evidence of your age, relationship, and marital status. It is strongly recommended that your Social Security earnings be verified with the Social Security Administration every three years. The statute of limitations for correcting your earnings record is three years, three months, and 15 days after the year in which the wages or self-employment income were earned.

Social Security offices can be reached at 1-800-772-1213. Representatives are available from 7AM to 7PM Monday through Friday. Recorded information is available 24 hours a day. Hearing impaired callers can call 1-800-325-0778. Social Security information and publications can also be obtained on the internet at http://www.ssa.gov.

Personal Financial Statement

Personal financial statements are commonly used by banks and other lending organizations when you are attempting to obtain credit. In some instances such as personal lines of credit, banks require this information to be updated annually. A personal financial statement contains information about your assets and liabilities, as well as your income and expenses.

Generally, lending institutions look at items such as your net worth (total assets minus total liabilities). They also look as different ratios such as percentage of monthly income needed for debt service. Consult your bank, lending institution, or financial advisor to find how to maximize the value an organization will place on your personal financial statement.

The following section represents a basic personal financial statement and its contents. As you will notice, the information on this form is very similar to the information requested in this book. After completing the related input forms, transfer the information to your personal financial statement. Doing this will give you a more definite picture of your overall financial situation.

Vantage Planning, LLC

The circumstances surrounding the death of a loved one can be one of the most difficult things you ever have to deal with. It can be absolutely overwhelming, especially when trying to deal with everything on your own. It was with this thought in mind that Vantage Planning, LLC was established.

The company is the nation's leader in assisting individuals in many different areas. First, they offer resources for helping people to get their estate in order so that everything is documented for their heirs. Additionally, they offer maintenance services by maintaining the documented information and make it available for your heirs upon your death. Another way they offer assistance is by sending periodic reminders of what information is on file and confirming the contents as well as asking if changes need to be made. This proves to be an invaluable tool for assisting both you and your family in times of need.

For more information on Vantage Planning, LLC and the services which they offer, request an information packet by filling out the card or call 888-338-9264.

Tax and Benefits Reference Material

The information included in this book can get you well on the way toward organizing your affairs for yourself and for your family. It is important that you take the time to complete the required information. While this book can be the best book you ever read, it is of no use to you unless you implement the information contained herein. Do not fall into the trap that the vast majority of people fall into. You are in control over how your estate is handled upon your death. Do what it takes. It is a decision which will not only change your life, but one which will serve as a gift to those you leave behind.

Form **1310** (Rev. March 1995) Department of the Treasury Internal Revenue Service

Statement of Person Claiming Refund Due a Deceased Taxpayer

► See instructions below and on back.

OMB No. 1545-0073

Attachment Sequence No. **87**

Tax year decedent was due a refund:
Calendar year ______ , or other tax year beginning ______ , 19 ___ , and ending ______ , 19 ___

Please type or print

Name of decedent	Date of death	**Decedent's social security number**
Name of person claiming refund		
Home address (number and street). If you have a P.O. box, see instructions.		Apt. no.
City, town or post office, state, and ZIP code. If you have a foreign address, see instructions.		

Part I **Check the box that applies to you.** Check only one box. **Be sure to complete Part III below.**

A ☐ Surviving spouse requesting reissuance of a refund check. See instructions.

B ☐ Court-appointed or certified personal representative. You may have to attach a court certificate showing your appointment. See instructions.

C ☐ Person, **other** than A or B, claiming refund for the decedent's estate. Also, complete Part II. You may have to attach a copy of the proof of death. See instructions.

Part II **Complete this part only if you checked the box on line C above.**

		Yes	No
1	Did the decedent leave a will?		
2a	Has a court appointed a personal representative for the estate of the decedent?		
b	If you answered **"No"** to 2a, will one be appointed?		
	If you answered **"Yes"** to 2a or 2b, the personal representative must file for the refund.		
3	As the person claiming the refund for the decedent's estate, will you pay out the refund according to the laws of the state where the decedent was a legal resident?		
	If you answered **"No"** to 3, a refund cannot be made until you submit a court certificate showing your appointment as personal representative or other evidence that you are entitled under state law to receive the refund.		

Part III **Signature and verification. All filers must complete this part.**

I request a refund of taxes overpaid by or on behalf of the decedent. Under penalties of perjury, I declare that I have examined this claim, and to the best of my knowledge and belief, it is true, correct, and complete.

Signature of person claiming refund ► **Date ►**

Paperwork Reduction Act Notice

We ask for the information on this form to carry out the Internal Revenue laws of the United States. You are required to give us the information. We need it to ensure that you are complying with these laws and to allow us to figure and collect the right amount of tax.

The time needed to complete and file this form will vary depending on individual circumstances. The estimated average time is:

Recordkeeping . . . . . 7 min.
Learning about the law or the form . . . . . 3 min.
Preparing the form . . . . . 16 min.
Copying, assembling, and sending the form to the IRS . . . . . 17 min.

If you have comments concerning the accuracy of these time estimates or suggestions for making this form simpler, we would be happy to hear from you. You can write to the **Internal Revenue Service,** Attention: Tax Forms Committee, PC:FP, Washington, DC 20224. **DO NOT** send the form to this address.

General Instructions

Purpose of Form

Use Form 1310 to claim a refund on behalf of a deceased taxpayer.

Who Must File

If you are claiming a refund on behalf of a deceased taxpayer, you must file Form 1310 unless **either** of the following applies:

- You are a surviving spouse filing an original or amended joint return with the decedent, OR
- You are a personal representative (see back of form) filing an original Form 1040, Form 1040A, Form 1040EZ, or Form 1040NR for the decedent and a court certificate showing your appointment is attached to the return.

Example. Assume Mr. Green died on January 4 before filing his tax return. On April 3 of the same year, you were appointed by the court as the personal representative for Mr. Green's estate and you file Form 1040 for Mr. Green. You do not need to file Form 1310 to claim the refund on Mr. Green's tax return. However, you must attach to his return a copy of the court certificate showing your appointment.

Cat. No. 11566B   Form **1310** (Rev. 3-95)

Personal Representative

For purposes of this form, a personal representative is the executor or administrator of the decedent's estate, as certified or appointed by the court. A copy of the decedent's will **cannot** be accepted as evidence that you are the personal representative.

Additional Information

For more details, see **Death of Taxpayer** in the index to the Form 1040, Form 1040A, or Form 1040EZ instructions, or get **Pub. 559,** Survivors, Executors, and Administrators.

Specific Instructions

P.O. Box

If your post office does not deliver mail to your home and you have a P.O. box, show your box number instead of your home address.

Foreign Address

If your address is outside the United States or its possessions or territories, enter the information on the line for "City, town or post office, state, and ZIP code" in the following order: city, province or state, postal code, and the name of the country. **Do not** abbreviate the country name.

Line A

Check the box on line A if you received a refund check in your name and your deceased spouse's name. You can return the joint-name check with Form 1310 to your local IRS office or the service center where you mailed your return. A new check will be issued in your name and mailed to you.

Line B

Check the box on line B **only** if you are the decedent's court-appointed personal representative claiming a refund for the decedent on **Form 1040X,** Amended U.S. Individual Income Tax Return, or **Form 843,** Claim for Refund and Request for Abatement. You **must** attach a copy of the court certificate showing your appointment. But if you have already sent the court certificate to the IRS, complete Form 1310 and write "Certificate Previously Filed" at the bottom of the form.

Line C

Check the box on line C if you are not a surviving spouse claiming a refund based on a joint return **and** there is no court-appointed personal representative. You must also complete Part II. If you check the box on line C, you **must** attach the proof of death. But if you have already sent the proof of death to the IRS, complete Form 1310 and write "Proof of Death Previously Filed" at the bottom of the form.

The proof of death **must** be an authentic copy of **either** of the following:

- The death certificate, or
- The telegram or letter from the Department of Defense notifying the next of kin of the decedent's death while in active service.

Example. Your father died on August 25. You are his sole survivor. Your father did not have a will and the court did not appoint a personal representative for his estate. Your father is entitled to a $300 refund. To get the refund, you must complete and attach Form 1310 to your father's final return. You should check the box on line C of Form 1310, answer all the questions in Part II, and sign your name in Part III. You must also attach a copy of the death certificate or other proof of death.

Lines 1-3

If you checked the box on line C, you must complete lines 1 through 3.

Million Heirs

Personal Financial Statement

A. General Information

Primary Applicant		Date Prepared	Spouse (if applicable)		Date Prepared
Social Security #	Home Phone	Date of Birth	Social Security #	Home Phone	Date of Birth
Position/Occupation	Business Name	Length of Employment	Position/Occupation	Business Name	Length of Employment
Business Address		Phone #	Business Address		Phone #

Current Address: No. Street	City	State	Zip	Length at present address

B. Assets and Liabilities

ASSETS		LIABILITIES	
Cash (checking, savings, CDs) - Sch E	$	Notes Payable to banks and others - Sch L	$
U.S Gov't & Marketable Securities - Sch F	$	Accounts Payable - Secured	
Non-Marketable Securities - Sch G	$	Accounts Payable - Unsecured	
Securities held by broker in margin accounts		Accounts and Bills Due	
Real Estate Owned - Sch H	$	Unpaid Income Tax	
Automobiles		Amounts due to brokers	
Accounts & Notes Receivable		Real Estate Mortgages Payable - Sch H	$
Cash surrender value of life insurance - Sch I	$	Other Liabilities - Itemize:	
Retirement and Profit sharing plans - Sch J	$		
Business ventures - Sch K	$		
Other Assets - Itemize:			
Total Assets:	**$**	**Total Liabilities:**	**$**
		Net Worth:	**$**

C. Annual Income and Expense

Annual Income	Individual	Joint	Annual Expenses	Individual	Joint
Salary & Commissions			Mortgage/rental pmts		
Interest & Dividends			Real Estate Taxes		
Real Estate Income			Income Taxes		
Other Income:			Insurance payments		
			Other Debt Service		
			Alimony, Child Support		
			Other Expenses:		
Total Annual Income:	**$**	**$**	**Total Expenses**	**$**	**$**

D. Personal Information

Have you or any business in which you were a major owner declared bankruptcy?	Y N	Do you have any contingent liabilities (as endorser, guarantor, et cetera)	Y N
Are you a defendant in a suit or legal action?	Y N	Do you have any other special debt?	Y N
Do you have any contested income tax liens?	Y N	Taxes have been filed and paid through what year?	

Personal Financial Statement

E. Cash (Checking, Savings, CDs)

Financial Institution	Owner	Type of Account	Balance

F. US Government & Marketable Securities

Description	Owner	# Shares	Balance

G. Non-Marketable Securities

Description	Owner	# Shares	Balance

H. Real Estate

Type of Investment (residence, rental, etc.)	Description/Location	Market Value	Unpaid Balance

I. Cash Surrender Value of Life Insurance

Insurance Company	Owner of Policy	Face Amount	Surrender Value

J. Retirement and Profit Sharing Plans

Company Name	Beneficiary	% Vested	Account Balance

K. Business Ventures

Company Name	Position/Title	% Ownership	Value of Investment

L. Notes Payable

Payable to:	Secured by:	Date Final Pmt	Present Balance

I (we) certify that the information contained in the statement has been read carefully and is correct, and complete to the best of my (our) belief.

Signature: ______________________

Date Signed: ______________________ Signature: ______________________

Notes

Notes

Notes

Appendix I
IRS Information

The key to becoming successful in anything you do is to gain as much knowledge in that area as possible. To do that, you need to constantly acquire new information and resources. One of the best places to get information when it comes to taxation and related issues is the Internal Revenue Service (IRS).

The IRS has numerous publications outlining their view on how things need to be taken care of. The Internal Revenue Service has spent millions and millions of dollars on publishing forms, booklets, and publications and making them readily available for taxpayers. I would tell you that these are all free, but unfortunately that is not the case. Now I don't mean that the IRS charges a fee for these, the reason I say that these are not free is because you have already paid for these resources with your tax dollars. Since you've already paid for these, it's time to get your copies.

There are a couple of ways to obtain the information. One way is to go to the local IRS office. However, a more convenient method may be to visit the IRS's website on the Internet at www.ustreas.gov. On the website, you can download copies of any forms you need. I have included one of the most important publications, Publication 559, in this book for your convenience.

Use the information in the publication and others to continually gain more and better knowledge. When taking care of your "million heirs," there's no such thing as too much preparation. Do what it takes to protect your family's future.

Department of the Treasury

Internal Revenue Service

Publication 559
Cat. No. 15107U

Survivors, Executors, and Administrators

For use in preparing

1997 Returns

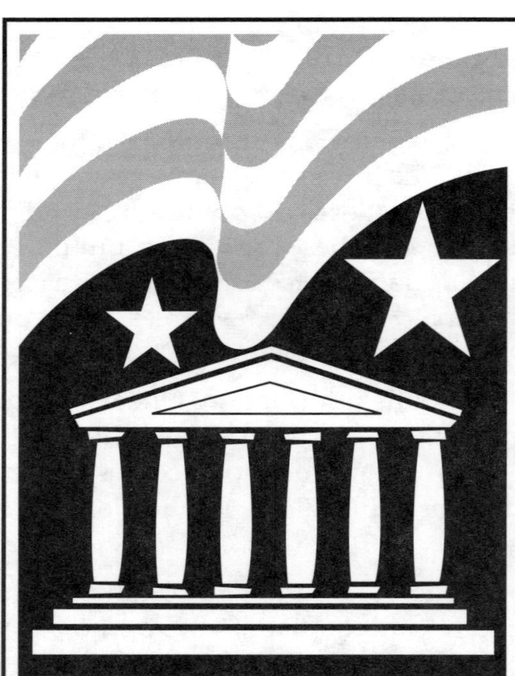

Get forms and other information faster and easier by:

COMPUTER
- World Wide Web ➤ www.irs.ustreas.gov
- FTP ➤ ftp.irs.ustreas.gov
- IRIS at FedWorld ➤ (703) 321-8020

FAX
- From your FAX machine, dial ➤ (703) 368-9694

See *How To Get More Information* in this publication.

Contents

Important Changes

Medical savings accounts (MSAs). Beginning in 1997, certain individuals are eligible to participate in medical savings accounts

(MSAs). For information on MSAs, see Publication 969, *Medical Savings Accounts (MSAs).*

The treatment of the MSA at the death of the account holder depends on who acquires the interest in the account. If the decedent's spouse is the designated beneficiary of the account, the account becomes the spouse's MSA. If another beneficiary (including a spouse that is not the designated beneficiary) acquires the interest, that person generally must include in gross income the fair market value of the assets in the account. If the decedent's estate acquires the interest, the fair market value of the assets in the account is included on the final income tax return of the decedent.

Accelerated death benefits. Beginning in 1997, certain payments received under a life insurance contract on the life of a terminally or chronically ill individual before the individual's death (an accelerated death benefit) can be excluded from income. For more information, see the discussion under *Income to Include,* under *Final Return for Decedent,* later.

Consistent treatment of estate and trust items. Beneficiaries must generally treat estate items the same way on their individual returns as they are treated on the estate's return. This rule applies to returns filed after August 5, 1997.

Estimated tax. Beginning in 1998, the estimated tax penalty will not apply unless the amount owed is $1,000 or more (up from $500). For more information, see *Estimated tax* later.

65–day rule for estates. For tax years beginning after August 5, 1997, the personal representative can elect to treat distributions paid or credited by the estate within 65 days after the close of the estate's tax year as having been paid or credited on the last day of that tax year.

Distributable net income. For purposes of determining distributable net income of the estate, the separate shares rule may apply if there is more than one beneficiary. This rule applies to estates of decedents dying after August 5, 1997. For more information, see *Distributions Deduction,* later.

Estates and beneficiaries treated as related persons for disallowance of certain items. For tax years beginning after August 5, 1997, an estate and a beneficiary of that estate are treated as related persons. Various tax provisions are affected by this change, including the one that denies a deduction for a loss on the sale of an asset between the parties.

The change does not apply to a sale or exchange made to satisfy a pecuniary bequest.

Survivor benefits of public safety officers. Generally, a survivor annuity paid to the spouse, former spouse, or child of a public safety officer killed in the line of duty is excluded from the recipient's gross income. This applies to officers dying after 1996.

Important Reminder

Individual taxpayer identification number (ITIN). The IRS will issue an ITIN to a nonresident or resident alien who does not have and is not eligible to get a social security number (SSN). To apply for an ITIN, file Form W-7 with the IRS. It usually takes 30 days to get it.

An ITIN is for tax use only. It does not entitle the holder to social security benefits or change the holder's employment or immigration status under U.S. law.

Introduction

This publication is designed to help those in charge of the property (estate) of an individual who has died. It shows them how to complete and file federal income tax returns and points out their responsibility to pay any taxes due.

A comprehensive example, using tax forms, is included near the end of this publication. Also included at the end of this publication are:

1) A checklist of the forms you may need and their due dates, and
2) A worksheet to reconcile amounts reported in the decedent's name on information Forms W–2, 1099–INT, 1099–DIV, etc. The worksheet will help you correctly determine the income to report on the decedent's final return and on the returns for either the estate or a beneficiary.

Useful Items

You may want to see:

Publication

- **950** Introduction to Estate and Gift Taxes

Form (and Instructions)

- **1040** U.S. Individual Income Tax Return
- **1041** U.S. Income Tax Return for Estates and Trusts
- **706** United States Estate (and Generation-Skipping Transfer) Tax Return

See *How To Get More Information,* near the end of this publication for information about getting these publications and forms.

Personal Representatives

A ***personal representative*** of an estate is an executor, administrator, or anyone who is in charge of the decedent's property. Generally, an ***executor*** (or executrix) is named in a decedent's will to administer the estate and distribute properties as the decedent has directed. An ***administrator*** (or administratrix) is usually appointed by the court if no will exists, if no executor was named in the will, or if the named executor cannot or will not serve.

In general, an executor and an administrator perform the same duties and have the same responsibilities.

For estate tax purposes, if there is no executor or administrator appointed, qualified, and acting within the United States, the term "executor" includes anyone in actual or constructive possession of any property of the decedent. It includes, among others, the decedent's agents and representatives; safe-deposit companies, warehouse companies, and other custodians of property in this country; brokers holding securities of the decedent as collateral; and the debtors of the decedent who are in this country.

Because a personal representative for a decedent's estate can be an executor, administrator, or anyone in charge of the decedent's property, the term "personal representative" will be used throughout this publication.

Duties

The primary duties of a personal representative are to collect all the decedent's assets, pay the creditors, and distribute the remaining assets to the heirs or other beneficiaries.

The personal representative also must:

1) File any income tax return and the estate tax return when due, and
2) Pay the tax determined up to the date of discharge from duties.

Other duties of the personal representative in federal tax matters are discussed in other sections of this publication. If any beneficiary is a nonresident alien, get Publication 515, *Withholding of Tax on Nonresident Aliens and Foreign Corporations,* for information on the personal representative's duties as a withholding agent.

Penalty. There is a penalty for failure to file a tax return when due unless the failure is due to reasonable cause. Relying on an agent (attorney, accountant, etc.) is not reasonable cause for late filing. It is the personal representative's duty to file the returns for the decedent and the estate when due.

Identification number. The first action you should take if you are the personal representative for the decedent is to apply for an ***employer identification number*** for the estate. You should apply for this number as soon as possible because you need to enter it on returns, statements, and other documents that you file concerning the estate. You must also give the number to payers of interest and dividends and other payers who must file a return concerning the estate. You must apply for the number on ***Form SS–4,*** *Application for Employer Identification Number,* available from IRS and Social Security Administration offices.

Payers of interest and dividends report amounts on Forms 1099 using the identification number of the person to whom the account is payable. After a decedent's death, the Forms 1099 must reflect the identification number of the estate or beneficiary to whom the amounts are payable. As the personal representative handling the estate you must furnish this identification number to the payer. For example, if interest is payable to the estate, the estate's identification number must be provided to the payer and used to report the interest on Form 1099–INT, *Interest Income.* If the interest is payable to a surviving joint owner, the survivor's identification number must be provided to the payer and used to report the interest.

The deceased individual's identifying number must not be used to file an individual tax return after the decedent's final tax return. It also must not be used to make estimated tax payments for a tax year after the year of death.

Penalty. If you do not include the employer identification number on any return, statement, or other document, you are liable for a penalty for each failure, unless you can show reasonable cause. You are also liable for a penalty if you do not give the employer identification number to another person, or if you do not include the taxpayer identification number of another person on a return, statement, or other document.

Notice of fiduciary relationship. The term "fiduciary" means any person acting for another person. It applies to persons who have positions of trust on behalf of others. A personal representative for a decedent's estate is a fiduciary.

If you are appointed to act in any fiduciary capacity for another, you must file a written notice with the IRS stating this. ***Form 56,*** *Notice Concerning Fiduciary Relationship,* can be used for this purpose. The instructions and other requirements are given on the back of the form.

Filing the notice. File the written notice (or Form 56) with the IRS service center where the returns are filed for the person (or estate) for whom you are acting. You should file this notice as soon as all of the necessary information (including the employer identification number) is available. It notifies the IRS that, as the fiduciary, you are assuming the powers, rights, duties, and privileges of the decedent, and allows the IRS to mail to you all tax notices concerning the person (or estate) you represent. The notice remains in effect until you notify the appropriate IRS office that your relationship to the estate has terminated.

Termination notice. When you are relieved of your responsibilities as personal representative, you must advise the IRS office where you filed the written notice (or Form 56) either that the estate has been terminated or that your successor has been appointed. If the estate is terminated, you must furnish satisfactory evidence of the termination of the estate. Use Form 56 for the termination notice by completing the appropriate part on the form and attaching the required evidence. If another has been appointed to succeed you as the personal representative, you should give the name and address of your successor.

Request for prompt assessment (charge) of tax. The IRS ordinarily has 3 years from the date an income tax return is filed, or its due date, whichever is later, to charge any additional tax that is due. However, as a personal representative you may request a prompt assessment of tax after the return has been filed. This reduces the time for making the assessment to 18 months from the date the written request for prompt assessment was received. This request can be made for any income tax return of the decedent and for the income tax return of the decedent's estate. This may permit a quicker settlement of the tax liability of the estate and an earlier final distribution of the assets to the beneficiaries.

Form 4810. Form 4810, *Request for Prompt Assessment Under Internal Revenue Code Section 6501(d),* can be used for making this request. It must be filed separately from any other document. The request should be filed with the IRS office where the return was filed. If Form 4810 is not used, you must clearly indicate that it is a request for prompt assessment under section 6501(d) of the Internal Revenue Code.

As the personal representative for the decedent's estate, you are responsible for any additional taxes that may be due. You can request prompt assessment of any taxes (other than federal estate taxes) for any open years for the decedent, even though the returns were filed before the decedent's death.

Failure to report income. If you or the decedent failed to report substantial amounts of gross income (more than 25% of the gross income reported on the return) or filed a false or fraudulent return, your request for prompt assessment will not shorten the period during which the IRS may assess the additional tax. However, such a request may relieve you of personal liability for the tax if you did not have knowledge of the unpaid tax.

Request for discharge from personal liability for tax. An executor can make a written request for a discharge from personal liability for a decedent's income and gift taxes. The request must be made after the returns for those taxes are filed. For this purpose an executor is an executor or administrator that is appointed, qualified, and acting within the United States.

Within 9 months after receipt of the request, the IRS will notify the executor of the amount of taxes due. If this amount is paid, the executor will be discharged from personal liability for any future deficiencies. If the IRS has not notified the executor, he or she will be discharged from personal liability at the end of the 9-month period.

CAUTION *Even if the executor is discharged, the IRS will still be able to assess tax deficiencies against the executor to the extent that he or she still has any of the decedent's property.*

Form 5495. Form 5495, *Request for Discharge from Personal Liability Under Internal Revenue Code Section 6905,* can be used for making this request. If Form 5495 is not used, you must clearly indicate that the request is for discharge from personal liability under section 6905 of the Internal Revenue Code.

Insolvent estate. If a decedent's estate is insufficient to pay all the decedent's debts, the debts due the United States must be paid first. Both the decedent's federal income tax liabilities at the time of death and the estate's income tax liability are debts due the United States. The personal representative of an insolvent estate is personally responsible for any tax liability of the decedent or of the estate if he or she had notice of such tax obligations or had failed to exercise due care in determining if such obligations existed before distribution of the estate's assets and before being discharged from duties. The extent of such personal responsibility is the amount of any other payments made before paying the debts due the United States. The income tax liabilities need not be formally assessed for the personal representative to be liable if he or she was aware or should have been aware of their existence.

Fees Received by Personal Representatives

All personal representatives must include in their gross incomes fees paid to them from an estate. If paid to a professional executor or administrator, self-employment tax also applies to such fees. For a nonprofessional executor or administrator (a person serving in such capacity in an isolated instance, such as a friend or relative of the decedent), self-employment tax only applies if a trade or business is included in the estate's assets, the executor actively participates in the business, and the fees are related to operation of the business.

Final Return for Decedent

The personal representative (defined earlier) must file the final income tax return of the decedent for the year of death and any returns not filed for preceding years. A surviving spouse, under certain circumstances, may have to file the returns for the decedent. See *Joint Return,* below.

Return for preceding year. If an individual died after the close of the tax year, but before the return for that year was filed, the return for the year just closed will not be the final return. The return for that year will be a regular return and the personal representative must file it.

Example. Samantha Smith died on March 21, 1997, before filing her 1996 tax return. Her personal representative must file her 1996 return by April 15, 1997. Her final tax return is due April 15, 1998.

Filing Requirements

The gross income, age, and filing status of a decedent generally determine whether a return must be filed. Gross income usually means money, goods, and property an individual received on which he or she must pay tax. It includes gross receipts from self-employment minus any cost of goods sold. It does not include nontaxable income. In general, filing status depends on whether the decedent was considered single or married at the time of death. See Publication 501, *Exemptions, Standard Deduction, and Filing Information.*

Refund

A return should be filed to obtain a refund if tax was withheld from salaries, wages, pensions, or annuities, or if estimated tax was paid, even if a return is not required to be filed. Also, the decedent may be entitled to other credits that result in a refund. These advance payments of tax and credits are discussed later under *Credits, Other Taxes, and Payments.*

Form 1310. Generally, a person who is filing a return for a decedent and claiming a refund must file a Form 1310, *Statement of Person Claiming Refund Due a Deceased Taxpayer,* with the return. However, if the person claiming the refund is a surviving spouse filing a joint return with the decedent, or a court-appointed or certified personal representative filing an original return for the decedent, Form 1310 is not needed. The personal representative must attach to the return a copy of the court certificate showing that he or she was appointed the personal representative.

Example. Assume that Mr. Green died on January 4, 1997, before filing his tax return. On April 3 of the same year, you were appointed the personal representative for Mr. Green's estate, and you filed his Form 1040 showing a refund due. You do not need Form 1310 to claim the refund if you attach a copy of the court certificate showing you were appointed the personal representative.

Nonresident Alien

If the decedent was a nonresident alien who would have had to file Form 1040NR, *U.S. Nonresident Alien Income Tax Return,* you must file that form for the decedent's final tax year. See the instructions for Form 1040NR for the filing requirements, due date, and where to file.

Joint Return

Generally, the personal representative and the surviving spouse can file a joint return for the decedent and the surviving spouse. However, the surviving spouse alone can file the joint return if no personal representative has been appointed before the due date for filing the final joint return for the year of death. This also applies to the return for the preceding year if the decedent died after the close of the preceding tax year and before the due date for filing that return. The income of the decedent that was includible on his or her return for the year up to the date of death (see *Income To Include,* later) and the income of the surviving spouse for the entire year must be included in the final joint return.

A final joint return with the deceased spouse cannot be filed if the surviving spouse remarried before the end of the year of the decedent's death. The filing status of the deceased spouse in this instance is "married filing separate return."

For information about tax benefits a surviving spouse may be entitled to, see *Tax Benefits for Survivors,* later under *Other Tax Information.*

Personal representative may revoke joint return election. A court-appointed personal representative may revoke an election to file a joint return that was previously made by the surviving spouse alone. This is done by filing a separate return for the decedent within one year from the due date of the return (including any extensions). The joint return made by the surviving spouse will then be regarded as the separate return of that spouse by excluding the decedent's items and refiguring the tax liability.

Income To Include

The decedent's income includible on the final return is generally determined as if the person were still alive except that the taxable period is usually shorter because it ends on the date of death. The method of accounting regularly used by the decedent before death also determines the income includible on the final return. This section explains how some types of income are reported on the final return.

For more information about accounting methods, get Publication 538, *Accounting Periods and Methods.*

Under the Cash Method

If the decedent accounted for income under the cash method, only those items actually or constructively received before death are accounted for in the final return.

Constructive receipt of income. Interest from coupons on the decedent's bonds was constructively received by the decedent if the coupons matured in the decedent's final tax year, but had not been cashed. Include the interest in the final return.

Generally, a dividend was constructively received if it was available for use by the decedent without restriction. If the corporation customarily mailed its dividend checks, the dividend was includible when received. If the individual died between the time the dividend was declared and the time it was received in the mail, the decedent did not constructively receive it before death. Do not include the dividend in the final return.

Under an Accrual Method

Generally, under an accrual method of accounting, income is reported when earned.

If the decedent used an accrual method, only the income items normally accrued before death are to be included in the final return.

Partnership Income

The death of a partner generally does not close the partnership's tax year before it normally ends. It continues for both the remaining partners and the deceased partner. Even if the partnership has only two partners, the death of one does not terminate the partnership or close its tax year, provided the deceased partner's estate or successor continues to share in the partnership's profits or losses. If the surviving partner terminates the partnership by discontinuing its business operations, the partnership tax year closes as of the date of termination. If the deceased partner's estate or successor sells, exchanges, or liquidates its entire interest in the partnership, the partnership's tax year for the estate or successor will close as of the date of the sale or exchange or the date the liquidation is completed.

On the decedent's final return include the decedent's distributive share of partnership income for the partnership's tax year ending within or with the decedent's last tax year (the year ending on the date of death).

Do not include on the final return the distributive share of partnership income for a partnership's tax year ending after the decedent's death. In this case, partnership income earned up to and including the date of death is income in respect of the decedent, discussed later. Income earned after the date of death to the end of the partnership's tax year is income to the estate or successor in interest.

Example. Mary Smith was a partner in XYZ partnership and reported her income on a tax year ending December 31. The partnership uses a tax year ending June 30. Mary died August 31, 1997, and her estate established its tax year ending August 31.

The distributive share of taxable income from the partnership based on the decedent's partnership interest is reported as follows:

1) Final Return for the Decedent — January 1 through August 31, 1997, includes income from the XYZ partnership year ending June 30, 1997.
2) Income Tax Return of the Estate — September 1, 1997, through August 31, 1998, includes income from the XYZ partnership year ending June 30, 1998. The portion of income from the partnership for the period July 1, 1997, through August 31, 1997, is income in respect of a decedent.

S Corporation Income

If the decedent was a shareholder in an S corporation, you must include on the final return the decedent's share of S corporation income for the corporation's tax year that ends within or with the decedent's last tax year (year ending on the date of death). The final return must also include the decedent's pro rata share of the S corporation's income for the period between the end of the corporation's last tax year and the date of death.

The income for the part of the S corporation's tax year after the shareholder's death is income to the estate or other person who has acquired the stock in the S corporation.

Self-Employment Income

Include self-employment income actually or constructively received or accrued, depending on the decedent's accounting method. For self-employment tax purposes only, the decedent's self-employment income will include the decedent's distributive share of a partnership's income or loss through the end of the month in which death occurred. For this purpose only, the partnership's income or loss is considered to be earned ratably over the partnership's tax year.

Community Income

If the decedent was married and was domiciled in a community property state, half of the income received and half of the expenses paid during the decedent's tax year by either the decedent or spouse may be considered to be the income and expenses of the other. For more information, get Publication 555, *Community Property.*

Interest and Dividend Income (Forms 1099)

A Form 1099 should be received for the decedent reporting interest and dividends that were includible on his or her return before death. A separate Form 1099 should be received showing the interest and dividends includible on the returns of the estate or other recipient after the date of death and payable to the estate or other recipient. You can request corrected Forms 1099, if these forms do not properly reflect the right recipient or amounts.

The amount reported on Form 1099–INT or Form 1099–DIV, *Dividends and Distributions,* may not necessarily be the correct amount that should be properly reported on each income tax return. For example, a Form 1099–INT reporting interest payable to a decedent may include income that should be reported on the final income tax return of the decedent, as well as income that the estate or other recipient should report, either as income earned after death or as income in respect of the decedent (discussed later). For income earned after death, you should ask the payer for a Form 1099 that properly identifies the recipient (by name and identification number) and the proper amount. If that is not possible, or if the form includes an amount that represents income in respect of the decedent, include an explanation, such as that shown next, under *How to report,* describing the amounts that are properly reported on the decedent's final return.

How to report. If you are preparing the decedent's final return and you have received a Form 1099–INT or a Form 1099–DIV for the decedent that includes amounts belonging to the decedent and to another recipient (the decedent's estate or another beneficiary), report the total interest shown on Form 1099–INT on Schedule 1 (Form 1040A) or on Schedule B (Form 1040). Next, enter a "subtotal" of the interest shown on Forms 1099, and the interest reportable from other sources for which you did not receive Forms 1099. Show any interest (including any interest you receive as a nominee) belonging to another recipient separately and subtract it from the subtotal. Identify the amount of this adjustment as "Nominee Distribution" or other appropriate designation. Report dividend income on the appropriate schedule using the same procedure.

Note. If the decedent received amounts as a nominee, you must give the actual owner a Form 1099, unless the owner is the decedent's spouse.

Medical Savings Account

The treatment of a medical savings account (MSA) at the death of the account holder depends on who acquires the interest in the account. If the estate of the holder acquires the interest, the fair market value of the assets in the account on the date of death is included in gross income on the decedent's final return. The estate tax deduction, discussed later, does not apply to this amount.

If a beneficiary acquires the interest, see the discussion under *Income in Respect of the Decedent,* later. For other information on MSAs, see Publication 969.

Accelerated Death Benefits

If certain requirements are met, accelerated death benefits are excluded from the recipient's income. Accelerated death benefits are amounts received under a life insurance contract before the death of the insured individual. These benefits also include amounts received on the sale or assignment of the contract to a viatical settlement provider. This exclusion applies only if the insured was a terminally or chronically ill individual.

Generally, if the decedent received accelerated death benefits either on his or her own life or on the life of another person, those benefits are not included in the decedent's income. For more information, see the discussion under *Gifts, Insurance, and Inheritances* under *Other Tax Information,* later.

Exemptions and Deductions

Generally, the rules for exemptions and deductions allowed to an individual also apply to the decedent's final income tax return. Show on the final return deductible items the decedent paid before death (or accrued, if the decedent reported deductions on an accrual method). This section contains a detailed discussion of medical expenses because, under certain conditions, the tax treatment can be different for the medical expenses of the decedent. See *Medical Expenses,* below.

Exemptions

You can claim the personal exemption in full on a final income tax return. If the decedent was another person's dependent (i.e., a parent's), you cannot claim the personal exemption on the decedent's final return.

Standard Deduction

If you do not itemize deductions on the final return, the full amount of the appropriate standard deduction is allowed regardless of the date of death. For information on the appropriate standard deduction, get Publication 501.

Medical Expenses

Medical expenses paid before death by the decedent are deductible on the final income tax return if deductions are itemized. This includes expenses for the decedent as well as for the decedent's spouse and dependents.

Qualified medical expenses paid before death by the decedent are not deductible if paid with a tax-free distribution from a medical savings account.

Election for decedent's expenses. Medical expenses that were not paid before death are liabilities of the estate and are shown on the federal estate tax return (Form 706). However, if medical expenses for the decedent are paid out of the estate during the 1–year period beginning with the day after death, you can elect to treat all or part of the expenses as paid by the decedent at the time they were incurred.

If you make the election, you can claim all or part of the expenses on the decedent's income tax return rather than on the federal estate tax return (Form 706). You can deduct expenses incurred in the year of death on the final income tax return. You should file an amended return (Form 1040X) for medical expenses incurred in an earlier year, unless the statutory period for filing a claim for that year has expired.

The amount you can deduct on the income tax return is the amount above 7.5% of adjusted gross income. The amounts not deductible because of this percentage cannot be claimed on the federal estate tax return.

Making the election. You make the election by filing with the decedent's income tax return, or amended return, a statement in duplicate that you have not claimed the amount as an estate tax deduction, and that the estate waives the right to claim the amount as a deduction. This election applies only to expenses incurred for the decedent, not to expenses incurred to provide medical care for dependents.

Example. Richard Brown used the cash method of accounting and filed his income tax return on a calendar year basis. Mr. Brown died on June 1, 1997, after incurring $800 in medical expenses. Of that amount, $500 was incurred in 1996 and $300 was incurred in 1997. Richard filed his 1996 income tax return before April 15, 1997. The personal representative of the estate paid the entire $800 liability in August 1997.

The personal representative may then file an amended return (Form 1040X) for 1996 claiming the $500 medical expense as a deduction, subject to the 7.5% limit. The $300 of expenses incurred in 1997 can be deducted on the final income tax return, subject to the 7.5% limit. The personal representative must file a statement in duplicate with each return stating that these amounts have not been claimed on the federal estate tax return (Form 706), and waiving the right to claim such a deduction on Form 706 in the future.

Medical expenses not paid by estate. If you paid medical expenses for your deceased spouse or dependent, claim the expenses on your tax return for the year in which you paid them, whether they are paid before or after the decedent's death. If the decedent was a child of divorced or separated parents, the medical expenses can usually be claimed by both the custodial and noncustodial parent to the extent paid by that parent during the year.

Insurance reimbursements. Insurance reimbursements of previously deducted medical expenses due a decedent at the time of death and later received by the decedent's estate are includible in the income tax return of the estate (Form 1041) for the year the reimbursements are received. The reimbursements are also includible in the decedent's gross estate.

Deduction for Losses

A decedent's net operating loss deduction from a prior year and any capital losses (capital losses include capital loss carryovers) can be deducted only on the decedent's final income tax return. A net operating loss on the decedent's final income tax return can be carried back to prior years.You cannot deduct any unused net operating loss or capital loss on the estate's income tax return.

At-risk loss limits. Special at-risk rules apply to most activities that are engaged in as a trade or business or for the production of income.

These rules limit the amount of deductible loss to the amount for which the individual was considered at risk in the activity. An individual generally will be considered at risk to the extent of the cash and the adjusted basis of property that he or she contributed to the activity and any amounts the individual borrowed for use in the activity. However, an individual will be considered at risk for amounts borrowed only if he or she was personally liable for the repayment or if the amounts borrowed were secured by property other than that used in the activity. The individual is not considered at risk for borrowed amounts if the lender has an interest in the activity or if the lender is related to a person who has an interest in the activity. For more information, get Publication 925, *Passive Activity and At-Risk Rules.*

Passive activity rules. A passive activity is any trade or business activity in which the taxpayer does not materially participate. To determine material participation, get Publication 925. Rental activities are also passive activities regardless of the taxpayer's participation, unless the taxpayer meets certain eligibility requirements.

Individuals, estates, and trusts can offset passive activity losses only against passive activity income. Passive activity losses or credits that are not allowed in one tax year can be carried forward to the next year.

In general, if a passive activity interest is transferred because of the death of a taxpayer, the accumulated unused passive activity losses are allowed as a deduction against the decedent's income in the year of death. Losses are allowed only to the extent they are greater than the excess of the transferee's (recipient of the interest transferred) basis in the property over the decedent's adjusted basis in the property immediately before death. The portion of the losses that is equal to the excess is not allowed as a deduction for any tax year.

Use Form 8582, *Passive Activity Loss Limitations,* to summarize losses and income from passive activities and to figure the amounts allowed. For more information, get Publication 925.

Credits, Other Taxes, and Payments

This section includes brief discussions of some of the tax credits, types of taxes that may be owed, income tax withheld, and estimated tax payments that are reported on the final return of a decedent.

Credits

You can claim on the final income tax return any tax credits that applied to the decedent before death. Some of these credits are discussed next.

Earned income credit. If the decedent was an eligible individual, you can claim the earned income credit on the decedent's final return even though the return covers less than 12 months. If the allowable credit is more than the tax liability for the year, the excess is refunded.

For more information, get Publication 596, *Earned Income Credit.*

Credit for the elderly or the disabled. This credit is allowable on a decedent's final income tax return if the decedent was age 65 or older or had retired before the end of the tax year on permanent and total disability.

For more information, get Publication 524, *Credit for the Elderly or the Disabled.*

General business tax credit. The general business credit available to a taxpayer is limited. Any unused credit generally is carried back 3 years and then carried forward for up to 15 years. After the 15–year period, a deduction may be allowed for any unused business credit. If the taxpayer dies before the end of the 15–year period, the deduction generally is allowed in the year of death.

For more information, get Publication 334, *Tax Guide for Small Business.*

Other Taxes

Taxes other than income tax that may be owed on the final return of a decedent include self-employment tax and alternative minimum tax, which are reported in the *Other Taxes* section of Form 1040.

Self-employment tax. If the decedent had net earnings from self-employment of $400 or more in the year of death, self-employment tax may be owed on the final return.

Alternative minimum tax (AMT). The tax laws give special treatment to some kinds of income and allow special deductions and credits for some kinds of expenses. So that taxpayers who benefit from these laws will pay at least a minimum amount of tax, a special tax has been enacted—the "alternative minimum tax" (AMT). In general, the AMT is the excess of the tentative minimum tax over the regular tax shown on the return.

Form 6251. Use Form 6251, *Alternative Minimum Tax—Individuals,* to determine if this tax applies to the decedent. See the form instructions for information on when you must attach the form to the tax return.

Payments of Tax

The income tax withheld from the decedent's salary, wages, pensions, or annuities, and the amount paid as estimated tax, for example, are credits (advance payments of tax) that you must claim on the final return.

Name, Address, and Signature

The word "DECEASED," the decedent's name, and the date of death should be written across the top of the tax return. In the name and address space you should write the name and address of the decedent and the surviving spouse. If a joint return is not being filed, the decedent's name should be written in the name space and the personal representative's name and address should be written in the remaining space.

Signature. If a personal representative has been appointed, that person must sign the return. If it is a joint return, the surviving spouse must also sign it. If no personal representative has been appointed, the surviving spouse (on a joint return) should sign the return and write in the signature area "Filing as surviving spouse." If no personal representative has been appointed and if there is no surviving spouse, the person in charge of the decedent's property must file and sign the return as "personal representative."

When and Where To File

The final individual income tax return is due at the same time the decedent's return would have been due had death not occurred. A final return for a decedent who was a calendar year taxpayer is generally due on April 15 following the year of death, regardless of when during the year death occurred. However, when the due date falls on a Saturday, Sunday, or legal holiday, you can file on the next business day.

The tax return must be prepared on a form for the year of death regardless of when during the year death occurred.

File the final income tax return of the decedent with the Internal Revenue Service center for the place where you live. You also may handcarry the return to any office of the district director within your district.

Tax Forgiveness for Deaths Due to Military or Terrorist Actions

If the decedent was a member of the Armed Forces or a civilian employee of the United States, the decedent's income tax liability may be forgiven if his or her death was due to service in a combat zone or to military or terrorist actions.

Combat Zone

If a member of the Armed Forces of the United States dies while in active service in a combat zone or from wounds, disease, or injury incurred in a combat zone, the decedent's income tax liability is abated (forgiven) for the entire year in which death occurred and for any prior tax year ending on or after the first day the person served in a combat zone in active service. For this purpose, a qualified hazardous duty area is treated as a combat zone.

If the tax (including interest, additions to the tax, and additional amounts) for these years has been assessed, the assessment will be forgiven. If the tax has been collected (regardless of the date of collection), that tax will be credited or refunded.

Any of the decedent's income tax for tax years before those mentioned above that remains unpaid as of the actual (or presumptive) date of death will not be assessed. If any unpaid tax (including interest, additions to the tax, and additional amounts) has been assessed, this assessment will be forgiven. Also, if any tax was collected after the date of death, that amount will be credited or refunded.

The date of death of a member of the Armed Forces reported as missing in action or as a prisoner of war is the date his or her name is removed from missing status for military pay purposes. This is true even if death actually occurred earlier.

Military or Terrorist Actions

The decedent's income tax liability is forgiven if, at death, he or she was a military or civilian employee of the United States who died because of wounds or injury incurred:

1) While a U.S. employee, and
2) In a military or terrorist action outside the United States.

The forgiveness applies to the tax year in which death occurred and for any prior tax year in the period beginning with the year before the year in which the wounds or injury occurred.

Example. The income tax liability of a civilian employee of the United States who died in 1997 because of wounds incurred while a U.S. employee outside the United States in a terrorist attack that occurred in 1987 will be forgiven for 1997 and for all prior tax years in the period 1986–1996. Refunds are allowed for the tax years for which the period for filing a claim for refund has not ended, as discussed later.

Military or terrorist action defined. Military or terrorist action means:

1) Any terrorist activity that most of the evidence indicates was directed against the United States or any of its allies, and
2) Any military action involving the U.S. Armed Forces and resulting from violence or aggression against the United States or any of its allies, or the threat of such violence or aggression.

Military action does not include training exercises. Any multinational force in which the United States is participating is treated as an ally of the United States.

Claim for Credit or Refund

If any of these tax-forgiveness situations applies to a prior year tax, any tax paid for which the period for filing a claim has not ended will be credited or refunded; if any tax is still due, it will be canceled. The normal period for filing a claim for credit or refund is 3 years after the return was filed or 2 years after the tax was paid, whichever is later.

If death occurred in a combat zone or from wounds, disease, or injury incurred in a combat zone, the period for filing the claim is extended by:

1) The amount of time served in the combat zone (including any period in which the individual was in missing status); plus
2) The period of continuous qualified hospitalization for injury from service in the combat zone, if any; plus
3) The next 180 days.

Qualified hospitalization means any hospitalization outside the United States, and any hospitalization in the United States of not more than 5 years.

Filing a claim. Use the following procedures to file a claim.

1) If a U.S. individual income tax return (Form 1040, 1040A, or 1040EZ) has not been filed, you should make a claim for refund of any withheld income tax or estimated tax payments by filing Form 1040, 1040A, or 1040EZ. Form W–2, *Wage and Tax Statement,* must accompany all returns.
2) If a U.S. individual income tax return has been filed, you should make a claim for refund by filing Form 1040X. You must file a separate Form 1040X for each year in question.

You must file these returns and claims with the Internal Revenue Service, P.O. Box 267, Covington, KY 41019, Attn: Stop 28.

Identify all returns and claims for refund by writing "Desert Storm — KIA "or "Former Yugoslavia — KIA "in bold letters on the top of page 1 of the return or claim. On Forms 1040 and 1040X, the phrase "Desert Storm — KIA "or "Former Yugoslavia — KIA "must be written on the line for "total tax. "If the individual was killed in a terroristic or military action outside the United States, put "KITA" on the front of the return and on the line for "total tax. "

An attachment should include a computation of the decedent's tax liability and a computation of the amount that is to be forgiven. On joint returns, you must make an allocation of the tax as described later under *Joint returns.* If you cannot make a proper allocation, you should attach a statement of all income and deductions allocable to each spouse and the IRS will make the proper allocation.

The following ***necessary documents*** must accompany all returns and claims for refund under these procedures:

1) Form 1310, *Statement of Person Claiming Refund Due a Deceased Taxpayer.*
2) A certification from the Department of Defense or the Department of State that the death was due to military or terrorist action outside the United States. For military employees and civilian employees of the Department of Defense, certification must be made by that department on Form DOD 1300. For civilian employees of all other agencies, certification must be a letter signed by the Director General of the Foreign Service, Department of State, or his/her delegate. The certification must include the individual's name and social security number, the date of injury, the date of death, and a statement that the individual died as the result of a military or terrorist action outside the United States and was an employee of the United States at the date of injury and at the date of death.

If the certification has been received, but you do not have enough tax information to file a timely claim for refund, you can suspend the period for filing a claim by filing Form 1040X, attaching Form 1310 and a statement that an amended claim will be filed as soon as you have the required tax information.

Joint returns. If a joint return was filed, only the decedent's part of the income tax liability is eligible for the refund. Determine the decedent's tax liability as follows:

1) Figure the income tax for which the decedent would have been liable if a separate return had been filed.
2) Figure the income tax for which the spouse would have been liable if a separate return had been filed.
3) Multiply the joint tax liability by a fraction. The numerator (top number) of the fraction is the amount in (1), above. The denominator (bottom number) of the fraction is the total of (1) and (2).

The amount in (3) above is the decedent's tax liability that is eligible for the refund.

Filing Reminders

To minimize the time needed to process the decedent's final return and issue any refund, be sure to follow these procedures:

1) Write "DECEASED," the decedent's name, and the date of death across the top of the tax return.
2) If a personal representative has been appointed, the personal representative must sign the return. If it is a joint return, the surviving spouse must also sign it.
3) If you are the decedent's spouse filing a joint return with the decedent and no personal representative has been appointed, write "Filing as surviving spouse "in the area where you sign the return.
4) If no personal representative has been appointed and if there is no surviving spouse, the person in charge of the decedent's property must file and sign the return as "personal representative."
5) To claim a refund for the decedent:
   a) If you are the decedent's spouse filing a joint return with the decedent, file only the tax return to claim the refund.
   b) If you are the personal representative and the return is not a joint return filed with the decedent's surviving spouse, file the return and attach a copy of the certificate that shows your appointment by the court. (A power of attorney or a copy of the decedent's will is not acceptable evidence of your appointment as the personal representative). If you are filing an amended return, attach Form 1310 and a copy of the certificate of appointment (or, if you have already sent the certificate of appointment to IRS, write "Certificate Previously Filed" at the bottom of Form 1310).
   c) If you are not filing a joint return as the surviving spouse and a personal representative has not been appointed, file the return and attach Form 1310 and proof of death (generally, a copy of the death certificate).

Other Tax Information

This section contains information about the effect of an individual's death on the income tax liability of the survivors (including widows and widowers), the beneficiaries, and the estate.

Your Federal Income Tax (Publication 17), published by the IRS, contains comprehensive information to help individual taxpayers prepare their own income tax returns. Also, there are many other taxpayer information publications on specific topics. You can get single copies of these publications free from the IRS Forms Distribution Center. See *How To Get More Information* near the end of this publication.

Tax Benefits for Survivors

Survivors can qualify for certain benefits when filing their own income tax returns.

Joint return by surviving spouse. A surviving spouse can file a joint return for the year of death and may qualify for special tax rates for the following 2 years, as explained under *Qualifying widows and widowers,* below.

Decedent as your dependent. If the decedent qualified as your dependent for the part of the year before death, you can claim the full exemption amount for the dependent on your tax return, regardless of when death occurred during the year.

Qualifying widows and widowers. If your spouse died within the 2 tax years preceding the year for which your return is being filed, you may be eligible to claim the filing status of qualifying widow(er) with dependent child and qualify to use the *Married filing jointly* tax rates.

Requirements. Generally, you qualify for this special benefit if you meet all of the following requirements:

1) You were entitled to file a joint return with your spouse for the year of death—whether or not you actually filed jointly;
2) You did not remarry before the end of the current tax year;
3) You have a child, stepchild, or foster child who qualifies as your dependent for the tax year; and
4) You provide more than half the cost of maintaining your home, which is the

principal residence of that child for the entire year except for temporary absences.

Example. William Burns's wife died in 1995. Mr. Burns has not remarried and continued throughout 1996 and 1997 to maintain a home for himself and his dependent child. For 1995 he was entitled to file a joint return for himself and his deceased wife. For 1996 and 1997, he qualifies to file as a "Qualifying widow(er) with dependent child." For later years, he may qualify to file as a head of household.

Figuring your tax. Include only your own income, exemptions, and deductions in figuring your tax, but check the box on line 5 (Form 1040 or 1040A) under filing status on your tax return and enter the year of death in the parentheses. Use the Tax Rate Schedule or the column in the Tax Table for *Married filing jointly,* which gives you the split-income benefits.

The last year you can file jointly with, or claim an exemption for, your deceased spouse is the year of death.

Joint return filing rules. If you are the surviving spouse and a personal representative is handling the estate for the decedent, you should coordinate filing your return for the year of death with this personal representative. See *Joint Return* earlier under *Final Return for Decedent.*

Income in Respect of the Decedent

All gross income that the decedent would have received had death not occurred, that was not properly includible on the final return, discussed earlier, is income in respect of the decedent.

How To Report

Income in respect of a decedent must be included in the gross income of:

1) The decedent's estate, if the estate receives it, or
2) The beneficiary, if the right to income is passed directly to the beneficiary and the beneficiary receives it, or
3) Any person to whom the estate properly distributes the right to receive it.

Example 1. Frank Johnson owned and operated an apple orchard. He used the cash method of accounting. He sold and delivered 1,000 bushels of apples to a canning factory for $2,000, but did not receive payment before his death. When the estate was settled, payment had not been made and the estate transferred the right to the payment to his widow. When Frank's widow collects the $2,000, she must include that amount in her return. It is not to be reported on the final return of the decedent nor on the return of the estate.

Example 2. Assume Frank Johnson used the accrual method of accounting in Example 1. The amount accrued from the sale of the apples would be included on his final return. Neither the estate nor the widow will realize income in respect of the decedent when the money is later paid.

Example 3. On February 1, George High, a cash method taxpayer, sold his tractor for $3,000, payable March 1 of the same year. His adjusted basis in the tractor was $2,000. Mr. High died on February 15, before receiving payment. The gain to be reported as income in respect of the decedent is the $1,000 difference between the decedent's basis in the property and the sale proceeds. In other words, the income in respect of the decedent is the gain the decedent would have realized had he lived.

Example 4. Cathy O'Neil was entitled to a large salary payment at the date of her death. The amount was to be paid in five annual installments. The estate, after collecting two installments, distributed the right to the remaining installments to you, the beneficiary. None of the payments would be included in Cathy's final return. The estate must include in its gross income the two installments it received, and you must include in your gross income each of the three installments as you receive them.

Example 5. You inherited the right to receive renewal commissions on life insurance sold by your father before his death. You inherited the right from your mother, who acquired it by bequest from your father. Your mother died before she received all the commissions she had the right to receive, so you received the rest. None of these commissions were included in your father's final return. But the commissions received by your mother were included in her gross income. The commissions you received are not includible in your mother's gross income, even on her final return. You must include them in your income.

Character of income. The character of the income you receive in respect of a decedent is the same as it would have been to the decedent if he or she were alive. If the income would have been a capital gain to the decedent, it will be a capital gain to you.

Transfer of right to income. If you transfer your right to income in respect of a decedent, you must include in your income the greater of:

1) The amount you receive for the right, or
2) The fair market value of the right you transfer.

If you make a gift of such a right, you must include in your gross income the fair market value of the right at the time of the gift.

If the right to income from an installment obligation is transferred, the amount you must include in income is reduced by the basis of the obligation. See *Installment obligations,* below.

Transfer defined. A transfer for this purpose includes a sale, exchange, or other disposition, the satisfaction of an installment obligation at other than face value, or the cancellation of an installment obligation.

Installment obligations. If the decedent had sold property using the installment method and you collect payments on an installment obligation you acquired from the decedent, use the same gross profit percentage the decedent used to figure the part of each payment that represents profit. Include in your income the same profit the decedent would have included had death not occurred. Get Publication 537, *Installment Sales.*

If you dispose of an installment obligation acquired from a decedent (other than by transfer to the obligor), the rules explained in Publication 537 for figuring gain or loss on the disposition apply to you.

Transfer to obligor. A transfer of a right to income, discussed earlier, has occurred if the decedent (seller) had sold property using the installment method and the installment obligation is transferred to the obligor (buyer or person legally obligated to pay the installments). A transfer also occurs if the obligation is canceled either at death or by the estate or person receiving the obligation from the decedent. An obligation that becomes unenforceable is treated as having been canceled.

If such a transfer occurs, the amount included in the income of the transferor (the estate or beneficiary) is the greater of the amount received or the fair market value of the installment obligation at the time of transfer, reduced by the basis of the obligation. The basis of the obligation is the decedent's basis, adjusted for all installment payments received after the decedent's death and before the transfer.

If the decedent and obligor were related persons, the fair market value of the obligation cannot be less than its face value.

Specific Types of Income in Respect of a Decedent

This section explains and provides examples of some specific types of income in respect of a decedent.

Wages. The entire amount of wages or other employee compensation earned by the decedent but unpaid at the time of death is income in respect of the decedent. The income is not reduced by any amounts withheld by the employer when paid to the estate or other beneficiary. If the income is $600 or more, the employer should report it in box 3 of Form 1099–MISC and give the recipient a copy of the form or a similar statement.

Wages paid as income in respect of a decedent are not subject to federal income tax withholding. However, if paid during the calendar year of death, they are subject to withholding for social security and Medicare taxes. These taxes should be included on the decedent's Form W–2 with the taxes withheld before death. Wages paid as income in respect of a decedent after the year of death generally are not subject to withholding for any federal taxes.

Farm income from crops, crop shares, and livestock. A farmer's growing crops and livestock at the date of death would not normally give rise to income in respect of a decedent or income to be included in the final return. However, when a cash method farmer receives rent in the form of crop shares or livestock and owns the crop shares or livestock at the time of death, the rent is income in respect of a decedent and is reported in the year in which the crop shares or livestock are sold or otherwise disposed of. The same treatment applies to crop shares or livestock the decedent had a right to receive as rent at the time of death for economic activities that occurred before death.

If the individual died during a rent period, only the portion of the proceeds from the portion of the rent period ending with death is income in respect of a decedent. The proceeds from the portion of the rent period from the day after death to the end of the rent period are income to the estate. Cash rent or crop shares and livestock received as rent and reduced to cash by the decedent are includible in the final return even though the rent period did not end until after death.

Example. Alonzo Roberts, who used the cash method of accounting, leased part of his farm for a 1–year period beginning March 1. The rental was one-third of the crop, payable in cash when the crop share is sold at the direction of Roberts. Roberts died on June 30 and was alive during 122 days of the rental period. Seven months later, Roberts' personal representative ordered the crop to be sold and was paid $1,500. Of the $1,500, 122/365, or $501, is income in respect of a decedent. The balance of the $1,500 received by the estate, $999, is income to the estate.

Partnership income. Any part of a distributive share of partnership income of the estate or other successor in interest of a deceased partner that is for the period ending with the date of the decedent's death is income in respect of a decedent. Any partnership income for the period after the decedent's death is income of the estate or other successor in interest. These rules apply to the partnership's tax year that ends after the date of the decedent's death. See *Partnership Income* under *Income To Include,* earlier in the section titled *Final Return for Decedent.*

If the partner who died had been receiving payments representing a distributive share or guaranteed payment in liquidation of the partner's interest in a partnership, the remaining payments made to the estate or other successor interest are income in respect of the decedent. The estate or the successor receiving the payments will have to include them in gross income when received. Similarly, the estate or other successor in interest receives income in respect of a decedent if amounts are paid by a third person in exchange for the successor's right to the future payments.

For a complete discussion of partnership rules, get Publication 541, *Partnerships.*

U.S. Savings Bonds acquired from decedent. If Series EE U.S. Savings Bonds that were owned by a cash method individual who had chosen to report the interest each year (or by an accrual method individual) are transferred because of death, the increase in value of the bonds (interest earned) in the year of death up to the date of death must be reported on the decedent's final return. The transferee (estate or beneficiary) reports on its return only the interest earned after the date of death.

The redemption values of U.S. Savings Bonds generally are available from local banks or savings and loan institutions. You also can get such information from your nearest Federal Reserve Bank; or you can purchase the *Tables of Redemption Values for U.S. Savings Bonds* from the Superintendent of Documents, U.S. Government Printing Office, Washington, D.C. 20402–9325.

If the bonds transferred because of death were owned by a cash method individual who had not chosen to report the interest each year and had purchased the bonds entirely with personal funds, interest earned before death must be reported in one of the following ways:

1) The person (executor, administrator, etc.) who must file the final income tax return of the decedent can ***elect*** to include in it all of the interest earned on the bonds before the decedent's death. The transferee (estate or beneficiary) then includes in its return only the interest earned after the date of death; or

2) If the election in (1), above, was not made, the interest earned to the date of death is income in respect of the decedent and is not included in the decedent's final return. In this case, all of the interest earned before and after the decedent's death is income to the transferee (estate or beneficiary). A transferee who uses the cash method of accounting and who has not chosen to report the interest annually may defer reporting any of it until the bonds are cashed or the date of maturity, whichever is earlier. In the year the interest is reported, the transferee may claim a deduction for any federal estate tax paid that arose because of the part of interest (if any) included in the decedent's estate.

Example 1. Your uncle, a cash method taxpayer, died and left you a $1,000 Series EE Bond. He had bought the bond for $500 and had not chosen to report the increase in value each year. At the date of death, interest of $94 had accrued on the bond, and its value of $594 at date of death was included in your uncle's estate. Your uncle's personal representative did not choose to include the $94 accrued interest in the decedent's final income tax return. You are a cash method taxpayer and do not choose to report the increase in value each year as it is earned. Assuming you cash it when it reaches maturity value of $1,000, you would report $500 interest income (the difference between maturity value of $1,000 and the original cost of $500) in that year. You also are entitled to claim, in that year, a deduction for any federal estate tax resulting from the inclusion in your uncle's estate of the $94 increase in value.

Example 2. If, in Example 1, the personal representative had chosen to include the $94 interest earned on the bond before death in the final income tax return of your uncle, you would report only $406 ($500 minus $94) as interest when you cashed the bond at maturity. Since this $406 represents the interest earned after your uncle's death and was not included in his estate, no deduction for federal estate tax is allowable for this amount.

Example 3. Your uncle died owning Series HH Bonds that he acquired in exchange for Series EE Bonds. You were the beneficiary on these bonds. The decedent used the cash method of accounting and had not chosen to report the increase in redemption price of the Series EE Bonds each year as it accrued. Your uncle's personal representative made no election to include any interest earned before death in the decedent's final return. Your income in respect of the decedent is the sum of the unreported increase in value of the Series EE Bonds, which constituted part of the amount paid for Series HH Bonds, and the interest, if any, payable on the Series HH Bonds but not received as of the date of the decedent's death.

Specific dollar amount legacy satisfied by transfer of bonds. If you receive Series EE Bonds from an estate in satisfaction of a specific dollar amount legacy and the decedent was a cash method taxpayer who did not elect to report interest each year, only the interest earned after you receive the bonds is your income. The interest earned to the date of death plus any further interest earned to the date of distribution is income to (and reportable by) the estate.

Cashing U.S. Savings Bonds. When you cash a U.S. Savings Bond that you acquired from a decedent, the bank or other payer that redeems it must give you a Form 1099–INT, *Interest Income,* if the interest part of the payment you receive is $10 or more. Your Form 1099–INT should show the difference between the amount received and the cost of the bond. The interest shown on your Form 1099–INT will not be reduced by any interest reported by the decedent before death, or, if elected, by the personal representative on the final income tax return of the decedent, or by the estate on the estate's income tax return. Your Form 1099–INT may show more interest than you must include in your income.

You must make an adjustment on your tax return to report the correct amount of interest. Get Publication 550, *Investment Income and Expenses,* for information about the correct reporting of this interest.

Interest accrued on U.S. Treasury bonds. The interest accrued on U.S. Treasury bonds owned by a cash method taxpayer and redeemable for the payment of federal estate taxes that was not received as of the date of the individual's death is income in respect of the decedent. This interest is not included in the decedent's final income tax return. The estate will treat such interest as taxable income in the tax year received if it chooses to redeem the U.S. Treasury bonds to pay federal estate taxes. If the person entitled to the bonds by bequest, devise, or inheritance, or because of the death of the individual (owner) receives them, that person will treat the accrued interest as taxable income in the year the interest is received. Interest that accrues on the U.S. Treasury bonds after the owner's death does not represent income in respect of the decedent. The interest, however, is taxable income and must be included in the gross income of the respective recipients.

Interest accrued on savings certificates. The interest accrued on savings certificates (redeemable after death without forfeiture of interest) that is for the period from the date of the last interest payment and ending with the date of the decedent's death, but not received as of that date, is income in respect of a decedent. Interest for a period after the decedent's death that becomes payable on the certificates after death is not income in respect of a decedent, but is taxable income includible in the gross income of the respective recipients.

Inherited IRAs. If a beneficiary receives a lump-sum distribution from an IRA he or she inherited, all or some of it may be taxable. The distribution is taxable in the year received as income in respect of a decedent up to the decedent's taxable IRA balance. This is the decedent's balance at the time of death, including unrealized appreciation and income accrued to date of death, minus any nontaxable basis (nondeductible contributions). Amounts distributed that are more than the decedent's entire IRA balance (includes taxable and nontaxable amounts) at the time of death are the income of the beneficiary.

If the beneficiary is the decedent's surviving spouse and that spouse properly rolls over the distribution into another IRA, the distribution is not currently taxed.

For the special rules on inherited IRAs, see Publication 590, *Individual Retirement Arrangements (IRAs) (Including SEP-IRAs and SIMPLE IRAs).*

Medical savings account (MSA). The treatment of an MSA at the death of the account holder depends on who acquires the interest in the account. If the decedent's estate acquired the interest, see the discussion under *Final Return for Decedent,* earlier.

If the decedent's spouse is the designated beneficiary of the MSA, the MSA becomes that spouse's MSA. It is subject to the rules discussed in Publication 969.

Any other beneficiary (including a spouse that is not the designated beneficiary) must include in gross income the fair market value of the assets in the account on the decedent's date of death. This amount must be reported for the beneficiary's tax year that includes the decedent's date of death. The amount included in gross income is reduced by the qualified medical expenses for the decedent that are paid by the beneficiary within 1 year after the decedent's date of death. An estate tax deduction, discussed later, applies to the amount included in income by a beneficiary, other than the decedent's spouse.

Deductions in Respect of the Decedent

Items such as business expenses, income-producing expenses, interest, and taxes, for which the decedent was liable but which are not properly allowable as deductions on the decedent's final income tax return, will be allowed when paid:

1) As a deduction to the estate; or

2) If the estate was not liable for them, as a deduction to the person who acquired an interest in the decedent's property (subject to such obligations) because of death.

Similar treatment is given to the foreign tax credit. A beneficiary who must pay a foreign tax on income in respect of a decedent will be entitled to claim the foreign tax credit.

Depletion. The deduction for percentage depletion is allowable only to the person (estate or beneficiary) who has an economic interest in respect of the decedent to which the deduction relates, whether or not that person receives the property from which the income is derived. An heir who (because of the decedent's death) receives income as a result of the sale of units of mineral by the decedent (who used the cash method) will be entitled to the depletion allowance for that income. If the decedent had not figured the deduction on the basis of percentage depletion, any depletion deduction to which the decedent was entitled at the time of death would be allowable on the decedent's final return, and no depletion deduction in respect of the decedent would be allowed anyone else.

For more information about depletion, get Publication 535, *Business Expenses.*

Estate Tax Deduction

Income that a decedent had a right to receive is included in the decedent's gross estate and is subject to estate tax. This income in respect of a decedent is also taxed when received by the recipient (estate or beneficiary). However, an income tax deduction is allowed to the recipient for the estate tax paid on the income.

The deduction for estate tax can be claimed only for the same tax year in which the income in respect of the decedent must be included in the recipient's gross income. (This also is true for income in respect of a prior decedent.)

Individuals can claim this deduction only as an itemized deduction, provided they are otherwise eligible to itemize deductions. This deduction is ***not*** subject to the 2% limit on miscellaneous itemized deductions. Estates can claim the deduction on the line provided for the deduction on Form 1041. For the alternative minimum tax computation, the deduction is not included in the itemized deductions that are an adjustment to taxable income.

If the income in respect of the decedent is capital gain income, for figuring the maximum tax on net capital gain (or any net capital loss limits), the gain must be reduced, but not below zero, by any deduction for estate tax paid on such gain.

Computation. To figure a recipient's estate tax deduction, determine—

1) The estate tax that qualifies for the deduction, and

2) The recipient's part of the deductible tax.

Deductible estate tax. The estate tax is the tax on the taxable estate, reduced by any credits allowed. The estate tax qualifying for the deduction is the part for the net value of all the items in the estate that represent income in respect of the decedent. ***Net value*** is the excess of the items of income in respect of the decedent over the items of expenses in respect of the decedent. The deductible estate tax is the difference between the actual estate tax and the estate tax determined without including net value.

Example 1. Jack Sage, an attorney who used the cash method of accounting, died in 1997. At the time of his death, he was entitled to receive $12,000 from clients for his services and he had accrued bond interest of $8,000, for a total income in respect of the decedent of $20,000. He also owed $5,000 for business expenses for which his estate was liable. The income and expenses were reported on Jack's estate tax return.

The tax on Jack's estate was $9,460 after credits. The net value of the items included as income in respect of the decedent is $15,000 ($20,000 minus $5,000). The estate tax determined without including the $15,000 in the taxable estate is $4,840, after credits. The estate tax that qualifies for the deduction is $4,620 ($9,460 minus $4,840).

Recipient's deductible part. Figure the recipient's part of the deductible estate tax by dividing the estate tax value of the items of income in respect of the decedent included in the recipient's gross income (the numerator) by the total value of all items included in the estate that represents income in respect of the decedent (the denominator). If the amount included in the recipient's gross income is less than the estate tax value of the item, use the lesser amount in the numerator.

Example 2. As the beneficiary of Jack's estate (Example 1, above), you collect the $12,000 accounts receivable from the clients during 1997. You will include this amount in your gross income for 1997. If you itemize your deductions for 1997, you can claim an estate tax deduction of $2,772 figured as follows:

$$\frac{\text{Value included in your income}}{\text{Total value of income in respect of decedent}} \times \text{Estate tax qualifying for deduction}$$

$$\frac{\$12,000}{\$20,000} \times \$4,620 = \$2,772$$

If the amount you collected for the accounts receivable was more than $12,000, you would still claim $2,772 as an estate tax deduction because only the $12,000 actually reported on the estate tax return can be used in the above computation. However, if you collected less than the $12,000 reported on the estate tax return, use the smaller amount to figure the estate tax deduction.

Estates. The estate tax deduction allowed an estate is figured in the same manner as just discussed. However, any income in respect of a decedent received by the estate during the tax year is reduced by any such income that is properly paid, credited, or required to be distributed by the estate to a beneficiary. The beneficiary would include such distributed income in respect of a decedent for figuring the beneficiary's deduction.

Surviving annuitants. For the estate tax deduction, an annuity received by a surviving annuitant under a joint and survivor annuity contract is considered income in respect of a decedent. The deceased annuitant must have died after the annuity starting date. You must make a special computation to figure the estate tax deduction for the surviving annuitant. See the Income Tax Regulations under Section 1.691(d)–1.

Gifts, Insurance, and Inheritances

Property received as a gift, bequest, or inheritance is not included in your income. But if property you receive in this manner later produces income, such as interest, dividends, or rentals, that income is taxable to you. The income from property donated to a trust that is paid, credited, or distributed to you is taxable income to you. If the gift, bequest, or inheritance is the income from property, that income is taxable to you.

If you receive property from a decedent's estate in satisfaction of your right to the income of the estate, it is treated as a bequest or inheritance of income from property. See *Distributions to Beneficiaries From an Estate,* later.

Insurance

The proceeds from a decedent's life insurance policy paid by reason of his or her death generally are excluded from income. The exclusion applies to any beneficiary, whether a family member or other individual, a corporation, or a partnership.

Veterans' insurance proceeds. Veterans' insurance proceeds and dividends are not taxable either to the veteran or to the beneficiaries.

Interest on dividends left on deposit with the Department of Veterans Affairs is not taxable.

Life insurance proceeds. Life insurance proceeds paid because of the death of the insured (or because the insured is a member of the U.S. uniformed services who is missing in action) are not taxable unless the policy was transferred to you for a valuable consideration. This rule also applies to benefits that are paid because of the death of the insured under accident, health, and variable life insurance policies and endowment contracts. However, if the proceeds are received in installments, see the discussion under *Insurance received in installments,* below.

Accelerated death benefits. Beginning in 1997, you can exclude from income accelerated death benefits you receive on the life of an insured individual if certain requirements are met. Accelerated death benefits are amounts received under a life insurance contract before the death of the insured. These benefits also include amounts received on the sale or assignment of the contract to a viatical settlement provider. This exclusion applies only if the insured was a terminally ill individual or a chronically ill individual. This exclusion does not apply if the insured is a director, officer, employee, or has a financial interest in any trade or business carried on by you.

Terminally ill individual. A terminally ill individual is an individual who has been certified by a physician as having an illness or physical condition that is expected to result in death in 24 months or less from the date of certification.

Chronically ill individual. A chronically ill individual is an individual who has been certified within the preceding 12–month period by a licensed health care practitioner as:

1) Being unable to perform (without help) at least two activities of daily living for at least 90 days due to a loss of functional capacity,

2) Having a level of disability similar to that described in (1), or

3) Requiring substantial supervision to protect the individual from threats to health and safety because of severe cognitive impairment.

Exclusion limited. If the insured was a chronically ill individual, your exclusion of accelerated death benefits is limited to the cost you incurred in providing qualified long-term care services for the insured. In determining the cost incurred do not include amounts paid or reimbursed by insurance or otherwise. Subject to certain limits, you can exclude payments received on a periodic basis without regard to your costs.

Insurance received in installments. If, because of the death of the insured, you will receive life insurance proceeds in installments, you can exclude a part of each installment from your income.

The part of each installment you can exclude is the amount held by the insurance company (generally, the total lump sum payable at the insured's death) divided by the number of periods in which the installments are to be paid. Amounts you receive that are more than the excludable part must be included in your income as interest income.

Specified number of installments. If you will receive a specified number of installments under the insurance contract, figure the part of each installment you can exclude by dividing the amount held by the insurance company by the number of installments to which you are entitled. A secondary beneficiary, in case you die before you receive all of the installments, is entitled to the same exclusion.

Example. As beneficiary, you choose to receive $40,000 of life insurance proceeds in 10 annual installments of $6,000. Each year, you can exclude from your gross income $4,000 ($40,000 √ 10) as a return of principal. The balance of the installment, $2,000, is taxable as interest income.

Specified amount payable. If each installment you receive under the insurance contract is a specific amount based on a guaranteed rate of interest, but the number of installments you will receive is uncertain, the part of each installment that you can exclude from income is the amount held by the insurance company divided by the number of installments necessary to use up the principal and guaranteed interest in the contract.

Example. The face amount of the policy is $150,000, and as beneficiary you choose to receive monthly installments of $1,250. The insurer's settlement option guarantees you this payment for 240 months based on a guaranteed rate of interest. It also provides that interest that is more than the guarantee may be credited to the principal balance according to the insurer's earnings. The excludable part of each guaranteed installment is $625 ($150,000 √ 240), or $7,500 for an entire year. The balance of each guaranteed installment, $625 (or $7,500 for a year), is income to you. The full amount of any additional payment for interest is income to you.

Installments for life. If, as the beneficiary under an insurance contract, you will receive the proceeds in installments for the rest of your life without a refund or certain guaranteed period, the part of each annual installment that you can exclude from income is the amount held by the insurance company, divided by your life expectancy. If the contract provides for a refund or guaranteed payments, the amount held by the insurance company for this calculation is reduced by the actuarial value of the refund or the guaranteed payments.

Example. As beneficiary, you choose to receive the $50,000 proceeds from a life insurance contract under a "life-income-with-cash-refund option." You are guaranteed $2,700 a year for the rest of your life (which is estimated by use of mortality tables to be 25 years from the insured's death). The actuarial value of the refund feature is $9,000. The amount held by the insurance company, reduced by the value of the guarantee, is $41,000 ($50,000 minus $9,000) and the excludable part of each installment representing a return of principal is $1,640 ($41,000 √ 25). The remaining $1,060 ($2,700 minus $1,640) is interest income to you. If you should die before receiving the entire $50,000, the refund payable to the refund beneficiary is not taxable.

Interest option on insurance. If death proceeds of life insurance are left on deposit with an insurance company under an agreement to pay interest only, the interest paid or credited to the beneficiary is taxable to the beneficiary.

Flexible premium contracts. A life insurance contract (including any qualified additional benefits) is a flexible premium life insurance contract if it provides for the payment of one or more premiums that are not fixed by the insurer as to both timing and amount. For contracts issued before January 1, 1985, the proceeds paid because of the death of the insured under a flexible premium contract will be excluded from the recipient's gross income only if the contracts meet the requirements explained under section 101(f) of the Internal Revenue Code.

Basis of Inherited Property

Your basis for property inherited from (or passing from) a decedent is generally one of the following:

1) The fair market value of the property at the date of the individual's death;

2) The fair market value on the alternate valuation date (discussed in the instructions for Form 706), if so elected by the personal representative for the estate; or

3) The value under the special-use valuation method for real property used in farming or other closely held business (see *Special-use valuation,* later), if so elected by the personal representative.

Exception for appreciated property. If you or your spouse gave ***appreciated property*** to an individual during the 1–year period ending on the date of that individual's death and you (or your spouse) later acquired the same property from the decedent, your basis in the property is the same as the decedent's adjusted basis immediately before death.

Appreciated property. Appreciated property is property with a fair market value greater than its adjusted basis on the day it was transferred to the decedent.

Special-use valuation. If you are a ***qualified heir*** and you receive a ***farm or other closely held business real property*** from the estate for which the personal representative elected special-use valuation, your basis is the value of the property on the basis of its actual use rather than its fair market value.

If you are a qualified heir and you buy special-use valuation property from the estate, your basis is the estate's basis (determined under the special-use valuation method) immediately before your purchase.

You are a ***qualified heir*** if you are an ancestor (parent, grandparent, etc.), the spouse, or a lineal descendant (child, grandchild, etc.) of the decedent, a lineal descendant of the decedent's parent or spouse, or the spouse of any of these lineal descendants.

For more information on special-use valuation, see Form 706.

Increased basis for special-use valuation property. Under certain conditions, some or all of the estate tax benefits obtained by using special-use valuation will be subject to recapture. If you must pay any additional estate (recapture) tax, you can elect to increase your basis in the special-use valuation property to its fair market value on the date of the decedent's death (or on the alternate valuation date, if the personal representative so elected).

If you elect to increase your basis, you must pay interest on the recapture tax for the period from the date 9 months after the decedent's death until the date you pay the recapture tax.

For more information on the recapture tax, see Form 706–A, *United States Additional Estate Tax Return.*

Adjusted basis for S corporation stock. The basis of inherited S corporation stock must be reduced if there is income in respect of a decedent attributable to that stock. This provision is effective with respect to decedents dying after August 20, 1996.

Joint interest. Figure the surviving tenant's new basis of property jointly owned (joint tenancy or tenancy by the entirety) by adding the surviving tenant's original basis in the property to the value of the part of the property (one of the three values described earlier) included in the decedent's estate. Subtract from the sum any deductions for wear and tear, such as depreciation or depletion, allowed to the surviving tenant on that property.

Example. Fred and Anne Maple (brother and sister) owned, as joint tenants with right of survivorship, rental property they purchased for $60,000. Anne paid $15,000 of the purchase price and Fred paid $45,000. Under local law, each had a half interest in the income from the property. When Fred died, the fair market value of the property was $100,000. Depreciation deductions allowed before Fred's death were $20,000. Anne's basis in the property is $80,000 figured as follows:

Anne's original basis	$15,000	
Interest acquired from Fred (¾ of $100,000)	75,000	$90,000
Minus: ½ of $20,000 depreciation		10,000
Anne's basis		$80,000

Qualified joint interest. One-half of the value of property owned by a decedent and spouse as tenants by the entirety, or as joint tenants with right of survivorship if the decedent and spouse are the only joint tenants, is included in the decedent's gross estate. This is true regardless of how much each contributed toward the purchase price.

Figure the basis for a surviving spouse by adding one-half of the property's cost basis to the value included in the gross estate. Subtract from this sum any deductions for wear and tear, such as depreciation or depletion, allowed on that property to the surviving spouse.

Example. Dan and Diane Gilbert owned, as tenants by the entirety, rental property they purchased for $60,000. Dan paid $15,000 of the purchase price and Diane paid $45,000. Under local law, each had a half interest in the income from the property. When Diane died, the fair market value of the property was $100,000. Depreciation deductions allowed before Diane's death were $20,000. Dan's basis in the property is $70,000 figured as follows:

One-half of cost basis (½ of $60,000)	$30,000	
Interest acquired from Diane (½ of $100,000)	50,000	$80,000
Minus: ½ of $20,000 depreciation		10,000
Dan's basis		$70,000

For more information about determining basis and adjusted basis in property, get Publication 551, *Basis of Assets.*

Community property state. If you and your spouse lived in a community property state, get Publication 551 for a discussion about figuring the basis of your community property after your spouse's death.

Depreciation. If you can depreciate property you inherited, you generally must use the modified accelerated cost recovery system (MACRS) to determine depreciation.

For joint interests and qualified joint interests, you must make two computations to figure depreciation: one for your original basis in the property and another for the inherited part of the property. Continue depreciating your original basis under the same method you had used in previous years. Depreciate the inherited part using MACRS.

For more information on MACRS, get Publication 946, *How To Depreciate Property.*

Substantial valuation misstatement. If the value or adjusted basis of any property claimed on an income tax return is 200% or more of the amount determined to be the correct amount, there is a substantial valuation misstatement. If this misstatement results in an underpayment of tax of more than $5,000, an addition to tax of 20% of the underpayment can apply. The penalty increases to 40% if the value or adjusted basis is 400% or more of the amount determined to be the correct amount. If the value shown on the estate tax return is overstated and you use that value as your basis in the inherited property, you could be liable for the addition to tax.

The IRS may waive all or part of the addition to tax if you have a reasonable basis for the claimed value. The fact that the adjusted basis on your income tax return is the same as the value on the estate tax return is not enough to show that you had a reasonable basis to claim the valuation.

Holding period. If you sell or dispose of inherited property that is a capital asset, you have a long-term gain or loss from property held for more than 18 months, regardless of how long you held the property.

Property distributed in kind. Your basis in property distributed in kind by a decedent's estate is the same as the estate's basis immediately before the distribution plus any gain, or minus any loss, recognized by the estate. Property is distributed in kind if it satisfies your right to receive another property or amount, such as the income of the estate or a specific dollar amount. Property distributed in kind generally includes any noncash property you receive from the estate other than:

1) A specific bequest (unless it must be distributed in more than three installments), or

2) Real property, the title to which passes directly to you under local law.

For information on an estate's recognized gain or loss on distributions in kind, see *Income To Include* under *Income Tax Return of an Estate–Form 1041,* later.

Other Items of Income

Some other items of income that you, as a survivor or beneficiary, may receive are discussed below. Lump-sum payments you receive as the surviving spouse or beneficiary of a deceased employee may represent accrued salary payments; distributions from employee profit-sharing, pension, annuity, and stock bonus plans; or other items that should be treated separately for tax purposes. The treatment of these lump-sum payments depends on what the payments represent.

Death benefit exclusion. If the decedent died before August 21, 1996, beneficiaries (or the estate) may qualify for the death benefit exclusion on employers' payments made because of an employee's (or, in some cases, a former employee's) death. The term "employee "includes a self-employed individual if the amounts are paid by a qualified trust or under a qualified plan.

The amount excluded from income with respect to any deceased employee cannot exceed $5,000 regardless of the number of employers or the number of beneficiaries. The exclusion applies whether there are one or more payments.

Example. Samuel Wilson was an officer in a corporation at the time of his death in July 1996. The board of directors voted to pay Sam's salary for the rest of the year to his widow in consideration of his past services. In January 1997, the corporation paid Mrs. Wilson a total of $38,000. The first $5,000 she received is excludable from her income, but she must include the balance of $33,000 on line 21, of her 1997 Form 1040. Had her husband died after August 20, 1996, Mrs. Wilson would not have been eligible for the exclusion.

Death benefit for public safety officers. The death benefit payable to surviving dependents of public safety officers (law enforcement officers or firefighters) who die as a result of traumatic injuries sustained in the line of duty is not included in either the beneficiaries' income or the decedent's gross estate. The benefit is administered through the Bureau of Justice Assistance (BJA).

The BJA can pay the surviving dependents an emergency interim benefit up to $3,000 if it determines that a public safety officer's death is one for which a benefit will probably be paid. If there is no final payment, the recipient of the interim benefit is liable for repayment. However, the BJA may waive all or part of the repayment if it will cause a hardship. If all or part of the repayment is waived, that amount is not included in gross income.

Survivor benefits of public safety officers. Generally, a survivor annuity paid to the spouse, former spouse, or child of a public safety officer killed in the line of duty is excluded from the recipient's gross income. The annuity must be provided under a government plan and is excludable to the extent that it is attributable to the officer's service as a public safety officer. For this purpose, public safety officers include police and law enforcement officers, fire fighters, ambulance crews, and rescue squads.

The exclusion does not apply if the recipient's actions were responsible for the officer's death. It also does not apply if:

- The death was caused by the intentional misconduct of the officer or by the officer's intention to cause such death,
- The officer was voluntarily intoxicated at the time of death, or
- The officer was performing his or her duties in a grossly negligent manner at the time of death.

This provision applies to officers dying after 1996.

Salary or wages. Salary or wages paid after the employee's death are usually taxable income to the beneficiary. See *Wages,* earlier, under *Specific Types of Income in Respect of a Decedent.*

Lump-sum distributions. You may be able to choose optional methods to figure the tax on lump-sum distributions from qualified employee retirement plans. For more information, get Publication 575, *Pension and Annuity Income.*

Pensions and annuities. For beneficiaries of deceased employees who receive pensions and annuities, get Publication 575. For beneficiaries of federal Civil Service employees, get Publication 721, *Tax Guide to U.S. Civil Service Retirement Benefits.*

Inherited IRAs. If a person other than the decedent's spouse inherits an IRA, that person cannot treat the IRA as one established on his or her behalf. If an IRA distribution is from contributions that were deducted or from earnings and gains in the IRA, it is fully taxable income. If there were nondeductible contributions, an allocation between taxable and nontaxable income must be made. (See *Inherited IRAs,* under *Income in Respect of the Decedent,* earlier, and Publication 590. The IRA cannot be rolled over into, or receive a rollover from, another IRA. No deduction is allowed for amounts paid into that inherited IRA. For more information about IRAs, get Publication 590.

Estate income. Estates may have to pay federal income tax. Beneficiaries may have to pay tax on their share of estate income. However, there is never a double tax. See *Distributions to Beneficiaries From an Estate,* later.

Income Tax Return of an Estate— Form 1041

An estate is a taxable entity separate from the decedent and comes into being with the death of the individual. It exists until the final distribution of its assets to the heirs and other beneficiaries. The income earned by the assets during this period must be reported by the estate under the conditions described in this publication. The tax generally is figured in the same manner and on the same basis as for individuals, with certain differences in the computation of deductions and credits, as explained later.

The estate's income, like an individual's income, must be reported annually on either a calendar or fiscal year basis. As the personal representative, you choose the estate's accounting period when you file its first Form 1041, *U.S. Income Tax Return for Estates and Trusts.* The estate's first tax year can be any period that ends on the last day of a month and does not exceed 12 months.

Once you choose the tax year, you cannot change it without IRS approval. Also, on the first income tax return, you must choose the accounting method (cash, accrual, or other) you will use to report the estate's income. Once you have used a method, you ordinarily cannot change it without IRS approval. For a more complete discussion of accounting periods and methods, get Publication 538, *Accounting Periods and Methods.*

Filing Requirements

Every domestic estate with gross income of $600 or more during a tax year must file a Form 1041. If one or more of the beneficiaries of the domestic estate are nonresident alien individuals, the personal representative must file Form 1041, even if the gross income of the estate is less than $600.

A fiduciary for a nonresident alien estate with U.S. source income, including any income that is effectively connected with the conduct of a trade or business in the United States, must file ***Form 1040NR,*** *U.S. Nonresident Alien Income Tax Return,* as the income tax return of the estate.

A nonresident alien who was a ***resident of Puerto Rico, Guam, American Samoa, or the Commonwealth of the Northern Mariana Islands*** for the entire tax year will, for this purpose, be treated as a resident alien of the United States.

Schedule K–1 (Form 1041)

As personal representative, you must file a separate Schedule K–1 (Form 1041), or an acceptable substitute (described below), for each beneficiary. File these schedules with Form 1041. You must show each beneficiary's taxpayer identification number. A $50 penalty is charged for each failure to provide the identifying number of each beneficiary unless reasonable cause is established for not providing it. When you assume your duties as the personal representative, you must ask each beneficiary to give you a taxpayer identification number. However, it is not required of a nonresident alien beneficiary who is not engaged in a trade or business within the United States or of an executor or administrator of the estate unless that person is also a beneficiary.

As personal representative, you must also furnish a Schedule K–1 (Form 1041), or a substitute, to the beneficiary by the date on which the Form 1041 is filed. Failure to provide this payee statement can result in a penalty of $50 for each failure. This penalty also applies if you omit information or include incorrect information on the payee statement.

You do not need prior approval for a ***substitute*** Schedule K–1 (Form 1041) that is an exact copy of the official schedule or that follows the specifications in Publication 1167, *Substitute Printed, Computer-Prepared, and Computer-Generated Tax Forms and Schedules.* You must have prior approval for any other substitute Schedule K–1 (Form 1041).

Beneficiaries. The personal representative has a fiduciary responsibility to the ultimate recipients of the income and the property of the estate. While the courts use a number of names to designate specific types of beneficiaries or the recipients of various types of property, it is sufficient in this publication to call all of them beneficiaries.

Liability of the beneficiary. The income tax liability of an estate attaches to the assets of the estate. If the income is distributed or must be distributed during the current tax year, it is reportable by each beneficiary on his or her individual income tax return. If the income does not have to be distributed, and is not distributed but is retained by the estate, the income tax on the income is payable by the estate. If the income is distributed later without the payment of the taxes due, the beneficiary can be liable for tax due and unpaid, to the extent of the value of the estate assets received.

Income of the estate is taxed to either the estate or the beneficiary, but not to both.

Nonresident alien beneficiary. As a resident or domestic fiduciary, in addition to filing Form 1041, you must file the return and pay the tax that may be due from a nonresident alien beneficiary. Depending upon a number of factors, you may or may not have to file Form 1040NR. For more information, get Publication 519, *U.S. Tax Guide for Aliens.*

You do not have to file the nonresident alien's return and pay the tax if that beneficiary has appointed an agent in the United States to file a federal income tax return. However, you must attach to the estate's return (Form 1041) a copy of the document that appoints the beneficiary's agent. You also must file Form 1042, *Annual Withholding Tax Return for U.S. Source Income of Foreign Persons,* in connection with income tax to be paid at the source on certain payments to nonresident aliens.

Amended Return

If you have to file an amended Form 1041, use a copy of the form for the appropriate year and check the "Amended return" box. Complete the entire return, correct the appropriate lines with the new information, and refigure the tax liability. On an attached sheet, explain the reason for the changes and identify the lines and amounts being changed.

If the amended return results in a change to income, or a change in distribution of any income or other information provided to a beneficiary, you must file an amended Schedule K–1 (Form 1041) and give a copy to each beneficiary. Check the "Amended K–1" box at the top of Schedule K–1.

Information Returns

Even though you may not have to file an income tax return for the estate, you may have to file Form 1099–DIV, *Dividends and Distributions,* Form 1099–INT, *Interest Income,* or Form 1099–MISC, *Miscellaneous Income,* if you receive the income as a nominee or middleman for another person. For more information on filing information returns, see the *Instructions for Forms 1099, 1098, 5498, and W-2G.*

You will not have to file information returns for the estate if the estate is the record owner and you file an income tax return for the estate on Form 1041 giving the name, address, and identifying number of each actual owner and furnish a completed Schedule K–1 (Form 1041) to each actual owner.

Penalty. A penalty of up to $50 can be charged for each failure to file or failure to include correct information on an information return. (Failure to include correct information includes failure to include all the information required and inclusion of incorrect information.) If it is shown that such failure is due to intentional disregard of the filing requirement, the penalty amount increases.

See the *Instructions for Forms 1099, 1098, 5498, and W–2G* for more information.

Two or More Personal Representatives

If property is located outside the state in which the decedent's home was located, more than one personal representative may be designated by the will or appointed by the court. The person designated or appointed to administer the estate in the state of the decedent's permanent home is called the ***domiciliary representative.*** The person designated or appointed to administer property in a state other than that of the decedent's permanent home is called an ***ancillary representative.***

Separate Forms 1041. Each representative must file a separate Form 1041. The domiciliary representative must include the estate's entire income in the return. The ancillary representative files with the appropriate IRS office for the ancillary's location. The ancillary representative should provide the following information on the return:

1) The name and address of the domiciliary representative;
2) The amount of gross income received by the ancillary representative; and
3) The deductions claimed against that income (including any income properly paid or credited by the ancillary representative to a beneficiary).

Estate of a nonresident alien. If the estate of a nonresident alien has a nonresident alien domiciliary representative and an ancillary representative who is a citizen or resident of the United States, the ancillary representative, in addition to filing a Form 1040NR to provide the information described in the preceding paragraph, must also file the return that the domiciliary representative otherwise would have to file.

Copy of the Will

You do not have to file a copy of the decedent's will unless requested by the IRS. If requested, you must attach a statement to it indicating the provisions that, in your opinion, determine how much of the estate's income is taxable to the estate or to the beneficiaries. You should also attach a statement signed by you under penalties of perjury that the will is a true and complete copy.

Income To Include

The estate's taxable income generally is figured the same way as an individual's income, except as explained in the following discussions.

Gross income of an estate consists of all items of income received or accrued during the tax year. It includes dividends, interest, rents, royalties, gain from the sale of property, and income from business, partnerships, trusts, and any other sources. For a discussion of income from dividends, interest, and other investment income and also gains and losses from the sale of investment property, get Publication 550. For a discussion of gains and losses from the sale of other property, including business property, get Publication 544, *Sales and Other Dispositions of Assets.*

If, as the personal representative, your duties include the operation of the decedent's business, get Publication 334. This publication explains the income, excise, and employment tax laws that apply to a sole proprietorship.

Income in respect of the decedent. As the personal representative of the estate, you may receive income that the decedent would have reported had death not occurred. For an explanation of this income, see *Income in Respect of the Decedent* under *Other Tax Information,* earlier. An estate may qualify to claim a deduction for estate taxes if the estate must include in gross income for any tax year an amount of income in respect of a decedent. See *Estate Tax Deduction,* earlier under *Other Tax Information* and its discussion *Deductions in Respect of the Decedent.*

Gain (or loss) from sale of property. During the administration of the estate, you may find it necessary or desirable to sell all or part of the estate's assets to pay debts and expenses of administration, or to make proper distributions of the assets to the beneficiaries. While you may have the legal authority to dispose of the property, title to it may be vested (given a legal interest in the property) in one or more of the beneficiaries. This is usually true of real property. To determine whether any gain or loss must be reported by the estate or by the beneficiaries, consult local law to determine the legal owner.

Redemption of stock to pay death taxes. Under certain conditions, a distribution to a shareholder (including the estate) in redemption of stock that was included in the decedent's gross estate may be allowed capital gain (or loss) treatment.

Character of asset. The character of an asset in the hands of an estate determines whether gain or loss on its sale or other disposition is capital or ordinary. The asset's character depends on how the estate holds or uses it. If it was a capital asset to the decedent, it generally will be a capital asset to the estate. If it was land or depreciable property used in the decedent's business and the estate continues the business, it generally will have the same character to the estate that it had in the decedent's hands. If it was held by the decedent for sale to customers, it generally will be considered to be held for sale to customers by the estate if the decedent's business continues to operate during the administration of the estate.

CAUTION *For tax years beginning after August 5, 1997, an estate and a beneficiary of that estate are generally treated as related persons for purposes of treating the gain on the sale of depreciable property between the parties as ordinary income. This does not apply to a sale or exchange made to satisfy a pecuniary bequest.*

Holding period. An estate (or other recipient) that acquires a capital asset from a decedent and sells or otherwise disposes of it is considered to have held that asset for more than 18 months, regardless of how long the asset is held.

Basis of asset. The basis used to figure gain or loss for property the estate receives from the decedent usually is its fair market value at the date of death, or at the alternate valuation date, if elected. Also see *Special-use valuation* under *Basis of Inherited Property* in the *Other Tax Information* section, earlier.

If the estate purchases property after the decedent's death, the basis generally will be its cost.

The basis of certain appreciated property the estate receives from the decedent will be the decedent's adjusted basis in the property immediately before death. This applies if the property was acquired by the decedent as a gift during the 1–year period before death, the property's fair market value on the date of the gift was greater than the donor's adjusted basis, and the proceeds of the sale of the property are distributed to the donor (or the donor's spouse).

Schedule D (Form 1041). To report gains (and losses) from the sale or exchange of capital assets by the estate, file Schedule D (Form 1041) with Form 1041. For additional information about the treatment of capital gains and losses, get the instructions for Schedule D (Form 1041).

Installment obligations. If an installment obligation owned by the decedent is transferred by the estate to the obligor (buyer or person obligated to pay) or is canceled at death, include the income from that event in the gross income of the estate. See *Installment obligations* under *Income in Respect of the Decedent* in the *Other Tax Information* section, earlier. Get Publication 537 for information about installment sales.

Gain from sale of special-use valuation property. If you elected special-use valuation for farm or other closely held business real property and that property is sold to a ***qualified heir,*** the estate will recognize gain on the sale if the fair market value on the date of the sale exceeds the fair market value on the date of the decedent's death (or on the alternate valuation date if it was elected).

Qualified heirs. Qualified heirs include the decedent's ancestors (parents, grandparents, etc.) and spouse, the decedent's lineal descendants (children, grandchildren, etc.) and their spouses, and lineal descendants (and their spouses) of the decedent's parents or spouse.

For more information about special-use valuation, get Form 706 and its instructions.

Gain from transfer of property to a political organization. Appreciated property that is transferred to a political organization is treated as sold by the estate. Appreciated property is property that has a fair market value (on the date of the transfer) greater than the estate's basis. The gain recognized is the difference between the estate's basis and the fair market value on the date transferred.

A political organization is any party, committee, association, fund, or other organization formed and operated to accept contributions or make expenditures for influencing the nomination, election, or appointment of an individual to any federal, state, or local public office.

Gain or loss on distributions in kind. An estate recognizes gain or loss on a distribution of property in kind to a beneficiary only in the following situations:

1) The distribution satisfies the beneficiary's right to receive either—
   a) A specific dollar amount (whether payable in cash, in unspecified property, or in both), or
   b) A specific property other than the property distributed.
2) You choose to recognize the gain or loss on the estate's income tax return.

The gain or loss is usually the difference between the fair market value of the property when distributed and the estate's basis in the property. But see *Gain from sale of special-use valuation property,* earlier, for a limit on the gain recognized on a transfer of such property to a qualified heir.

If you choose to recognize gain or loss, the choice applies to all noncash distributions during the tax year except charitable distributions and specific bequests. To make the choice, report the gain or loss on a Schedule D (Form 1041) attached to the estate's Form 1041 and check the box on line 7 in the *Other Information* section of Form 1041. You must make the choice by the due date (including extensions) of the estate's income tax return for the year of distribution. You must get the consent of the IRS to revoke the choice.

For more information, see *Property distributed in kind* under *Distributions Deduction,* later.

Exemption and Deductions

In figuring taxable income, an estate is generally allowed the same deductions as an individual. Special rules, however, apply to some deductions for an estate. This section includes discussions of those deductions affected by the special rules.

Exemption Deduction

An estate is allowed an exemption deduction of $600 in figuring its taxable income. No exemption for dependents is allowed to an estate. Even though the first return of an estate may be for a period of less than 12 months, the exemption is $600. If, however, the estate was given permission to change its accounting period, the exemption is $50 for each month of the short year.

Contributions

An estate qualifies for a deduction for amounts of gross income paid or permanently set aside for qualified charitable organizations. The adjusted gross income limits for individuals do not apply. However, to be deductible by an estate, the contribution must be specifically provided for in the decedent's will. If there is no will, or if the will makes no provision for the payment to a charitable organization, then a deduction will not be allowed even though all of the beneficiaries may agree to the gift.

You cannot deduct any contribution from income that is not included in the estate's gross income. If the will specifically provides that the contributions are to be paid out of the estate's gross income, the contributions are fully deductible. However, if the will contains no specific provisions, the contributions are considered to have been paid and are deductible in the same proportion as the gross income bears to the total of all classes of income.

For more information about contributions, get Publication 526, *Charitable Contributions,* and Publication 561, *Determining the Value of Donated Property.*

Losses

Generally, an estate can claim a deduction for a loss that it sustains on the sale of property. If an estate has a loss from the sale of property (other than stock) to a personal representative of such estate, it also can claim a loss deduction.

For a discussion of an estate's recognized loss on a distribution of property in kind to a beneficiary, see *Income To Include,* earlier.

For tax years beginning after August 5, 1997, an estate and a beneficiary of that estate are generally treated as related persons for purposes of the disallowance of a loss on the sale of an asset between related persons. The disallowance does not apply to a sale or exchange made to satisfy a pecuniary bequest.

Net operating loss deduction. An estate can claim a net operating loss deduction, figured in the same way as an individual's, except that it cannot deduct any distributions to beneficiaries (discussed later) or the deduction for charitable contributions in figuring the loss or the loss carryover. For a discussion of the carryover of an unused net operating loss to a beneficiary upon termination of the estate, see *Termination of Estate,* later, and get Publication 536, *Net Operating Losses.*

Casualty and theft losses. Losses incurred for casualty and theft during the administration of the estate can be deducted only if they have not been claimed on the federal estate tax return (Form 706). You must file a statement with the estate's income tax return waiving the deduction for estate tax purposes. See *Administration Expenses,* below.

The same rules that apply to individuals apply to the estate, except that in figuring the adjusted gross income of the estate used to figure the deductible loss, you deduct any administration expenses claimed. Get Form 4684, *Casualties and Thefts,* and its instructions to figure any loss deduction.

Carryover losses. Carryover losses resulting from net operating losses or capital losses sustained by the decedent ***before death*** cannot be deducted on the estate's income tax return.

Administration Expenses

Expenses of administering an estate can be deducted either from the gross estate in figuring the federal estate tax on Form 706 or from the estate's gross income in figuring the estate's income tax on Form 1041. However, these expenses cannot be claimed for ***both*** estate tax and income tax purposes. In most cases, this rule also applies to expenses incurred in the sale of property by an estate (not as a dealer).

To prevent a double deduction, amounts otherwise allowable in figuring the decedent's taxable estate for federal estate tax on Form 706 will not be allowed as a deduction in figuring the income tax of the estate or of any other person unless the personal representative files a statement, in duplicate, that the items of expense, as listed in the statement, have not been claimed as deductions for federal estate tax purposes and that all rights to claim such deductions are ***waived.*** One deduction or part of a deduction can be claimed for income tax purposes if the appropriate statement is filed, while another deduction or part is claimed for estate tax purposes. Claiming a deduction in figuring the estate income tax is not prevented when the same deduction is claimed on the estate tax return, so long as the estate tax deduction is not finally allowed and the preceding statement is filed. The statement can be filed at any time before the expiration of the statute of limitations that applies to the tax year for which the deduction is sought. This waiver procedure also applies to casualty losses incurred during administration of the estate.

Accrued expenses. The rules preventing double deductions do not apply to deductions for taxes, interest, business expenses, and other items accrued at the date of death. These expenses are allowable as a deduction for estate tax purposes as claims against the estate and also are allowable as deductions in respect of a decedent for income tax purposes. Deductions for interest, business expenses, and other items not accrued at the date of the decedent's death are allowable only as a deduction for administration expenses for both estate and income tax purposes and do not qualify for a double deduction.

Expenses allocable to tax-exempt income. When figuring the estate's taxable income on Form 1041, you cannot deduct administration expenses allocable to any of the estate's tax-exempt income. However, you can deduct these administration expenses when figuring the taxable estate for federal estate tax purposes on Form 706.

Depreciation and Depletion

The allowable deductions for depreciation and depletion that accrue after the decedent's death must be apportioned between the estate and the beneficiaries, depending on the income of the estate that is allocable to each.

Example. In 1997 the decedent's estate realized $3,000 of business income during the administration of the estate. The personal representative distributed $1,000 of the income to the decedent's son Ned and $2,000 to another son, Bill. The allowable depreciation on the business property is $300. Ned can take a deduction of $100 (($1,000 √ $3,000) $300), and Bill can take a deduction of $200 (($2,000 √ $3,000) $300).

Distributions Deduction

An estate is allowed a deduction for the tax year for any income that must be distributed currently and for other amounts that are properly paid or credited, or that must be distributed to beneficiaries. The deduction is limited to the ***distributable net income*** of the estate.

For special rules that apply in figuring the estate's distribution deduction, see *Special Rules for Distributions* under *Distributions to Beneficiaries From an Estate,* later.

Distributable net income. Distributable net income (determined on Schedule B of Form 1041) is the estate's income available for distribution. It is the estate's taxable income, with the following modifications:

Distributions to beneficiaries. Distributions to beneficiaries are not deducted.

Estate tax deduction. The deduction for estate tax on income in respect of the decedent is not allowed.

Personal exemption. No personal exemption deduction is allowed.

Capital gains. Capital gains ordinarily are not included in distributable net income. However, you include them in distributable net income if:

1) The gain is allocated to income in the accounts of the estate or by notice to the beneficiaries under the terms of the will or by local law;
2) The gain is allocated to the corpus or principal of the estate and is actually distributed to the beneficiaries during the tax year;
3) The gain is used, under either the terms of the will or the practice of the personal representative, to determine the amount that is distributed or must be distributed; or
4) Charitable contributions are made out of capital gains.

Capital losses. Capital losses are excluded in figuring distributable net income unless they enter into the computation of any capital gain that is distributed or must be distributed during the year.

Tax-exempt interest. Tax-exempt interest, including exempt-interest dividends, though excluded from the estate's gross income, is included in the distributable net income, but is reduced by:

1) The expenses that were not allowed in computing the estate's taxable income because they were attributable to tax-exempt interest (see *Expenses allocable to tax-exempt income* under *Administration Expenses,* earlier); and
2) The part of the tax-exempt interest deemed to have been used to make a charitable contribution. See *Contributions,* earlier.

The total tax-exempt interest earned by an estate must be shown in the *Other Information* section of the Form 1041. The beneficiary's part of the tax-exempt interest is shown on the Schedule K–1, Form 1041.

Separate shares rule. For estates of decedents dying after August 5, 1997, the separate shares rule applies if the estate has more than one beneficiary and the beneficiaries have substantially separate and independent shares. Under this rule, the separate shares are treated as separate estates for the sole purpose of determining the distributable net income allocable to a beneficiary.

There are separate shares if the governing instrument (the will and applicable state law) creates a separate economic interest for one beneficiary that is not affected by an economic interest of another beneficiary. An economic interest is a right to income or gains from specified items or property.

Example. A separate share in an estate would exist where the decedent's will provides that all shares in a closely-held corporation and the dividends paid on those shares go to only one beneficiary, and that such dividends would not affect any other amounts that any beneficiary is entitled to under the will. In this situation, the separate share in the dividends is treated as a separate estate for determining distributable net income based only on those dividends. Any other income of the estate is treated as a separate estate for determining distributable net income based on that other income.

Income that must be distributed currently. The distributions deduction includes any amount of income that, under the terms of the decedent's will or by reason of local law, must be distributed currently. This includes an amount that may be paid out of income or corpus (such as an annuity) to the extent it is paid out of income for the tax year. The deduction is allowed to the estate even if the personal representative does not make the distribution until a later year or makes no distribution until the final settlement and termination of the estate.

Support allowances. The distribution deduction includes any support allowance that, under a court order or decree or local law, the estate must pay the decedent's surviving spouse or other dependent for a limited period during administration of the estate. The allowance is deductible as income that must be distributed currently or as any other amount paid, credited, or required to be distributed, as discussed next.

Any other amount paid, credited, or required to be distributed. Any other amount paid, credited, or required to be distributed is allowed as a deduction to the estate only in the year actually paid, credited, or distributed. If there is no specific requirement by local law or by the terms of the will that income earned by the estate during administration be distributed currently, a deduction for distributions to the beneficiaries will be allowed to the estate, but only for the actual distributions during the tax year.

If the personal representative has discretion as to when the income is distributed, the deduction is allowed only in the year of distribution.

For tax years beginning after August 5, 1997, the personal representative can elect to treat distributions paid or credited within 65 days after the close of the estate's tax year as having been paid or credited on the last day of that tax year.

Alimony and separate maintenance. Alimony and separate maintenance payments that must be included in the spouse's or former spouse's income may be deducted as income that must be distributed currently if they are paid, credited, or distributed out of the income of the estate for the tax year. That spouse or former spouse is treated as a beneficiary.

Payment of beneficiary's obligations. Any payment made by the estate to satisfy a legal obligation of any person is deductible as income that must be distributed currently or as any other amount paid, credited, or required to be distributed. This includes a payment made to satisfy the person's obligation under local law to support another person, such as the person's minor child. The person whose obligation is satisfied is treated as a beneficiary of the estate.

This does not apply to a payment made to satisfy a person's obligation to pay alimony or separate maintenance.

The value of an interest in real estate. The value of an interest in real estate owned by a decedent, title to which passes directly to the beneficiaries under local law, is not included as any other amount paid, credited, or required to be distributed.

Property distributed in kind. If an estate distributes property in kind, the estate's deduction ordinarily is the lesser of its basis in the property or the property's fair market value when distributed. However, the deduction is the property's fair market value if the estate recognizes gain on the distribution. See *Gain or loss on distributions in kind* under *Income To Include,* earlier.

Property is distributed in kind if it satisfies the beneficiary's right to receive another property or amount, such as the income of the estate or a specific dollar amount. It generally includes any noncash distribution other than:

1) A specific bequest (unless it must be distributed in more than three installments), or
2) Real property, the title to which passes directly to the beneficiary under local law.

Character of amounts distributed. If the decedent's will or local law does not provide for the allocation of different classes of income, you must treat the amount deductible for distributions to beneficiaries as consisting of the same proportion of each class of items entering into the computation of distributable net income as the total of each class bears to the total distributable net income. For more information about the character of distributions, see *Character of Distributions* under *Distributions to Beneficiaries From an Estate,* later.

Example. An estate has distributable net income of $2,000, consisting of $1,000 of taxable interest and $1,000 of rental income. Distributions to the beneficiary total $1,500. The distribution deduction consists of $750 of taxable interest and $750 of rental income, unless the will or local law provides a different allocation.

Limit on deduction for distributions. You cannot deduct any amount of distributable net income not included in the estate's gross income.

Example. An estate has distributable net income of $2,000, consisting of $1,000 of dividends and $1,000 of tax-exempt interest. Distributions to the beneficiaries are $1,500. Except for this rule, the distribution deduction would be $1,500 ($750 of dividends and $750 of tax-exempt interest). However, as the result of this rule, the distribution deduction is limited to $750, because no deduction is allowed for the tax-exempt interest distributed.

Funeral and Medical Expenses

No deduction can be taken for funeral expenses or medical and dental expenses on the estate's income tax return, Form 1041.

Funeral expenses. Funeral expenses paid by the estate are not deductible in figuring the estate's taxable income on Form 1041. They are deductible only for determining the taxable estate for federal estate tax purposes on Form 706.

Medical and dental expenses of a decedent. The medical and dental expenses of a decedent paid by the estate are not deductible in figuring the estate's taxable income on Form 1041. You can deduct them in figuring the taxable estate for federal estate tax purposes on Form 706. If these expenses are paid within the 1–year period beginning with the day after the decedent's death, you can elect to deduct them on the decedent's income tax return (Form 1040) for the year in which they were incurred. See *Exemptions and Deductions* under *Final Return for Decedent,* earlier.

Credits, Tax, and Payments

This section includes brief discussions of some of the tax credits, types of taxes that may be owed, and estimated tax payments that are reported on the income tax return of the estate, Form 1041.

Credits

Estates generally are allowed the same tax credits that are allowed to individuals. The credits generally are allocated between the estate and the beneficiaries. However, estates are not allowed the credit for the elderly or the disabled or the earned income credit discussed earlier under *Final Return for Decedent.*

Foreign tax credit. Foreign tax credit is discussed in Publication 514, *Foreign Tax Credit for Individuals.*

General business credit. The general business credit is available to an estate that is involved in a business. For more information, get Publication 334.

Tax

An estate cannot use the Tax Table that applies to individuals. The tax rate schedule to use is in the instructions for Form 1041.

Alternative minimum tax (AMT). An estate may be liable for the alternative minimum tax. To figure the alternative minimum tax, use Schedule I (Form 1041), *Alternative Minimum Tax.* Certain credits may be limited by any "tentative minimum tax" figured on line 38, Part III of Schedule I (Form 1041), even if there is no alternative minimum tax liability.

If the estate takes a deduction for distributions to beneficiaries, complete Part I and Part II of Schedule I even if the estate does not owe alternative minimum tax. Allocate the income distribution deduction figured on a minimum tax basis among the beneficiaries and report each beneficiary's share on Schedule K–1 (Form 1041). Also show each beneficiary's share of any adjustments or tax preference items for depreciation, depletion, and amortization.

For more information, get the instructions to Form 1041.

Payments

The estate's income tax liability must be paid in full when the return is filed. You may have to pay estimated tax, however, as explained next.

Estimated tax. Estates with tax years ending 2 or more years after the date of the decedent's death must pay estimated tax in the same manner as individuals.

If you must make estimated tax payments for 1998, use ***Form 1041–ES,*** *Estimated Income Tax for Estates and Trusts,* to determine the estimated tax to be paid.

Generally, you must pay estimated tax if the estate is expected to owe, after subtracting any withholding and credits, at least $1,000 in tax for 1998. You will not, however, have to pay estimated tax if you expect the withholding and credits to be at least:

1) 90% of the tax to be shown on the 1998 return, or
2) 100% of the tax shown on the 1997 return (assuming the return covered all 12 months).

The percentage in (2) above is 110% if the estate's 1997 adjusted gross income (AGI) was $150,000 or more. To figure the estate's AGI, see the instructions for line 15b, Form 1041.

The general rule is that you must make your first estimated tax payment by April 15, 1998. You can either pay all of your estimated tax at that time or pay it in four equal amounts that are due by April 15, 1998; June 15, 1998; September 15, 1998; and January 15, 1999. For exceptions to the general rule, get the instructions for Form 1041–ES and Publication 505.

If your return is on a fiscal year basis, your due dates are the 15th day of the 4th, 6th, and 9th months of your fiscal year and the 1st month of the following fiscal year.

If any of these dates fall on a Saturday, Sunday, or legal holiday, use the next business day.

You may be charged a penalty for not paying enough estimated tax or for not making the payment on time in the required amount (even if you have an overpayment on your tax return). Get Form 2210, *Underpayment of Estimated Tax by Individuals, Estates, and Trusts,* to figure any penalty.

For more information, get the instructions for Form 1041–ES and Publication 505.

Name, Address, and Signature

In the top space of the name and address area of Form 1041, enter the exact name of the estate from the Form SS–4 used to apply for the estate's employer identification number. In the remaining spaces, enter the name and address of the personal representative (fiduciary) of the estate.

Signature. The personal representative (or its authorized officer if the personal representative is not an individual) must sign the return. An individual who prepares the return for pay must manually sign the return as preparer. Signature stamps or labels are not acceptable. For additional information about the requirements for preparers of returns, see the instructions for Form 1041.

When and Where To File

When you file Form 1041 (or Form 1040NR if it applies) depends on whether you choose a calendar year or a fiscal year as the estate's accounting period. Where you file Form 1041 depends on where you, as the personal representative, live or have your principal office.

When to file. If you choose the calendar year as the estate's accounting period, the Form 1041 for 1997 is due by April 15, 1998 (June 15, 1998, in the case of Form 1040NR for a nonresident alien estate that does not have an office in the United States). If you choose a fiscal year, the Form 1041 is due by the 15th day of the 4th month (6th month in the case of Form 1040NR) after the end of the tax year. If the due date is a Saturday, Sunday, or legal holiday, the return is due on the next business day.

Extension of time to file. An extension of time to file Form 1041 may be granted if you have clearly described the reasons that will cause your delay in filing the return. Use Form 2758, *Application for Extension of Time To File Certain Excise, Income, Information, and Other Returns,* to request an extension. The extension is not automatic, so you should request it early enough for the IRS to act on the application before the regular due date of Form 1041. You should file Form 2758 in duplicate with the IRS office where you must file Form 1041.

If you have not yet established an accounting period, filing Form 2758 will serve to establish the accounting period stated on that form. Changing to another accounting period requires prior approval of the IRS.

Generally, an extension of time to file a return ***does not extend the time for payment of tax due.*** You must pay the total income tax estimated to be due on Form 1041 in full by the regular due date of the return. For additional information, see the instructions for Form 2758.

Where to file. As the personal representative of an estate, file the estate's income tax return (Form 1041) with the Internal Revenue Service center for the state where you live or have your principal place of business. A list of the states and addresses that apply is in the instructions for Form 1041.

You must send Form 1040NR to the Internal Revenue Service center, Philadelphia, PA 19255.

Electronic filing. Form 1041 can be filed electronically or on magnetic tape. See the instructions for Form 1041 for more information.

Distributions to Beneficiaries From an Estate

If you are the beneficiary of an estate that must distribute all its income currently, you must report your share of the distributable net income whether or not you have actually received it.

If you are the beneficiary of an estate that does not have to distribute all its income currently, you must report all income that must be distributed to you (whether or not actually distributed) plus all other amounts paid, credited, or required to be distributed to you, up to your share of distributable net income. Distributable net income (figured without the charitable deduction) is the income of the estate available for distribution. As explained earlier in *Distributions Deduction* under *Income Tax Return of an Estate–Form 1041* and its discussion, *Exemption and Deductions,* for an amount to be currently distributable income, there must be a specific requirement for current distribution either under local law or by the terms of the decedent's will. If there is no such requirement, the income is reportable only when distributed.

Income That Must Be Distributed Currently

Beneficiaries who are entitled to receive currently distributable income generally must include in gross income the entire amount due them. However, if the currently distributable income is more than the estate's distributable net income figured without deducting charitable contributions, each beneficiary must include in gross income a ratable part of the distributable net income.

Example. Under the terms of the will of Gerald Peters, $5,000 a year is to be paid to his widow and $2,500 a year is to be paid to his daughter out of the estate's income during the period of administration. There are no charitable contributions. For the year, the estate's distributable net income is only $6,000. Since the distributable net income is less than the currently distributable income, the widow must include in her gross income only $4,000 ([5,000 √ 7,500] $6,000), and the daughter must include in her gross income only $2,000 ([2,500 √ 7,500] $6,000).

Annuity payable out of income or corpus. Income that must be distributed currently includes any amount that must be paid out of income or corpus (principal of the estate) to the extent the amount is satisfied out of income for the tax year. An annuity that must be paid in all events (either out of income or corpus) would qualify as income that must be distributed currently to the extent there is income of the estate not paid, credited, or required to be distributed to other beneficiaries for the tax year.

Example 1. Henry Frank's will provides that $500 be paid to the local Community Chest out of the income each year. It also provides that $2,000 a year is currently distributable out of income to his brother, Fred, and an annuity of $3,000 is to be paid to his sister, Sharon, out of income or corpus. Capital gains are allocable to corpus, but all expenses are to be charged against income. Last year, the estate had income of $6,000 and expenses of $3,000. The personal representative paid the $500 to the Community Chest and made the distributions to Fred and Sharon as required by the will.

The estate's distributable net income (figured before the charitable contribution) is $3,000. The currently distributable income totals $2,500 ($2,000 to Fred and $500 to Sharon). The income available for Sharon's annuity is only $500 because the will requires that the charitable contribution be paid out of current income. Because the $2,500 treated as distributed currently is less than the $3,000 distributable net income (before the contribution), Fred must include $2,000 in his gross income, and Sharon must include $500 in her gross income.

Example 2. Assume the same facts as in Example 1 except that the estate has an additional $1,000 of administration expenses, commissions, etc., that are chargeable to corpus. The estate's distributable net income (figured before the charitable contribution) is now $2,000 ($3,000 minus $1,000 additional expense). The amount treated as currently distributable income is still $2,500 ($2,000 to Fred and $500 to Sharon). Because the $2,500, treated as distributed currently, is more than the $2,000 distributable net income, Fred has to include only $1,600 ([2,000 √ 2,500] $2,000) in his gross income and Sharon has to include only $400 ([500 √ 2,500] $2,000) in her gross income. Because Fred and Sharon are beneficiaries of amounts that must be distributed currently, they do not benefit from the reduction of distributable net income by the charitable contribution deduction.

Other Amounts Distributed

Any other amount paid, credited, or required to be distributed to the beneficiary for the tax year also must be included in the beneficiary's gross income. Such an amount is in addition to those amounts that must be distributed currently, as discussed earlier. It does not include gifts or bequests of specific sums of money or specific property if such sums are paid in three or fewer installments. However, amounts that can be paid only out of income are not excluded under this rule. If the sum of the income that must be distributed currently and other amounts paid, credited, or required to be distributed exceeds distributable net income, these other amounts are included in the beneficiary's gross income only to the extent distributable net income exceeds the income that must be distributed currently. If there is more than one beneficiary, each will include in gross income only a pro rata share of such amounts.

For tax years beginning after August 5, 1997, the personal representative can elect to treat distributions paid or credited by the estate within 65 days after the close of the estate's tax year as having been paid or credited on the last day of that tax year.

Examples of other amounts paid are:

1) Distributions made at the discretion of the personal representative;
2) Distributions required by the terms of the will upon the happening of a specific event;
3) Annuities that must be paid in any event, but only out of corpus (principal);
4) Distributions of property in kind as defined earlier in *Distributions Deduction* under *Income Tax Return of an Estate–Form 1041* and its discussion, *Exemption and Deductions;* and
5) Distributions required for the support of the decedent's surviving spouse or other dependent for a limited period, but only out of corpus (principal).

If an estate distributes property in kind, the amount of the distribution ordinarily is the lesser of the estate's basis in the property or the property's fair market value when distributed. However, the amount of the distribution is the property's fair market value if the estate recognizes gain on the distribution. See *Gain or loss on distributions in kind* in the discussion *Income To Include* under *Income Tax Return of an Estate–Form 1041,* earlier.

Example. The terms of Michael Scott's will require the distribution of $2,500 of income annually to his wife, Susan. If any income remains, it may be accumulated or distributed to his two children, Joe and Alice, in amounts at the discretion of the personal representative. The personal representative also may invade the corpus (principal) for the benefit of Scott's wife and children.

Last year, the estate had income of $6,000 after deduction of all expenses. Its distributable net income is also $6,000. The personal representative distributed the required $2,500 of income to Susan. In addition, the personal representative distributed $1,500 each to Joe and Alice and an additional $2,000 to Susan.

Susan includes in her gross income the $2,500 of currently distributable income. The other amounts distributed totaled $5,000 ($1,500 + $1,500 + $2,000) and are includible in the income of Susan, Joe, and Alice to the extent of $3,500 (distributable net income of $6,000 minus currently distributable income to Susan of $2,500). Susan will include an additional $1,400 ([2,000 √ 5,000] $3,500) in her gross income. Joe and Alice each will include $1,050 ([1,500 √ 5,000] $3,500) in their gross incomes.

Discharge of a Legal Obligation

If an estate, under the terms of a will, discharges a legal obligation of a beneficiary, the discharge is included in that beneficiary's income as either currently distributable income or other amount paid. This does not apply to the discharge of a beneficiary's obligation to pay alimony or separate maintenance.

The beneficiary's legal obligations include a legal obligation of support, for example, of a minor child. Local law determines a legal obligation of support.

Character of Distributions

An amount distributed to a beneficiary for inclusion in gross income retains the same character for the beneficiary that it had for the estate.

No charitable contributions are made. If no charitable contributions are made during the tax year, you must treat the distributions as consisting of the same proportion of each class of items entering into the computation of distributable net income as the total of each class bears to the total distributable net income. Distributable net income was defined earlier in *Distributions Deduction* under *Income Tax Return of an Estate–Form 1041* and its discussion, *Exemption and Deductions.* However, if the will or local law specifically provides or requires a different allocation, you must use that allocation.

Example 1. An estate has distributable net income of $3,000, consisting of $1,800 in rents and $1,200 in taxable interest. There is no provision in the will or local law for the allocation of income. The personal representative distributes $1,500 each to Jim and Ted, beneficiaries under their father's will. Each will be treated as having received $900 in rents and $600 of taxable interest.

Example 2. Assume in Example 1 that the will provides for the payment of the taxable interest to Jim and the rental income to Ted and that the personal representative distributed the income under those provisions. Jim is treated as having received $1,200 in taxable interest and Ted is treated as having received $1,800 of rental income.

If a charitable contribution is made. If a charitable contribution is made by an estate and the terms of the will or local law provide for the contribution to be paid from specified sources, that provision governs. If no provision or requirement exists, the charitable contribution deduction must be allocated among the classes of income entering into the computation of the income of the estate before allocation of other deductions among the items of distributable net income. In allocating items of income and deductions to beneficiaries to whom income must be distributed currently, the charitable contribution deduction is not taken into account to the extent that it exceeds income for the year reduced by currently distributable income.

Example. The will of Harry Thomas requires a current distribution out of income of $3,000 a year to his wife, Betty, during the administration of the estate. The will also provides that the personal representative, using discretion, may distribute the balance of the current earnings either to Harry's son, Tim, or to one or more of certain designated charities. Last year, the estate's income consisted of $4,000 of taxable interest and $1,000 of tax-exempt interest. There were no deductible expenses. The personal representative distributed the $3,000 to Betty, made a contribution of $2,500 to the local heart association, and paid $1,500 to Tim.

The distributable net income for determining the character of the distribution to Betty is $3,000. The charitable contribution deduction to be taken into account for this computation is $2,000 (the estate's income ($5,000) minus the currently distributable income ($3,000)). The $2,000 charitable contribution deduction must be allocated: $1,600 ([4,000 √ 5,000] $2,000) to taxable interest and $400 ([1,000 √ 5,000] $2,000) to tax-exempt interest. Betty is considered to have received $2,400 ($4,000 minus $1,600) of taxable interest and $600 ($1,000 minus $400) of tax-exempt interest. She must include the $2,400 in her gross income. She must report the $600 of tax-exempt interest, but it is not taxable.

To determine the amount to be included in the gross income of Tim, however, take into account the entire charitable contribution deduction. Since the currently distributable income is greater than the estate's income after taking into account the charitable contribution deduction, none of the amount paid to Tim must be included in his gross income for the year.

How and When To Report

How you report your income from the estate depends on the character of the income in the hands of the estate. When you report the income depends on whether it represents amounts credited or required to be distributed to you or other amounts.

How to report estate income. Each item of income keeps the same character in your hands as it had in the hands of the estate. If the items of income distributed or considered to be distributed to you include dividends, tax-exempt interest, or capital gains, they will keep the same character in your hands for purposes of the tax treatment given those items. Report your dividends on line 9, Form 1040, and report your capital gains on Schedule D (Form 1040). The tax-exempt interest, while not included in taxable income, must be shown on line 8b, Form 1040. Report business and other nonpassive income on Schedule E, Part III (Form 1040).

The estate's personal representative should provide you with the classification of the various items that make up your share of the estate income and the credits you should take into consideration so that you can properly prepare your individual income tax return. See *Schedule K–1 (Form 1041),* later.

When to report estate income. If income from the estate is credited or must be distributed to you for a tax year, report that income (even if not distributed) on your return for that year. Report other income from the estate on your return for the year in which you receive it. If your tax year is different from the estate's tax year, see *Different tax years,* next.

Different tax years. You must include your share of the estate income in your return for your tax year in which the last day of the estate tax year falls. If the tax year of the estate is the calendar year and your tax year is a fiscal year ending on June 30, you will include in gross income for the tax year ended June 30 your share of the estate's distributable net income distributed or considered distributed during the calendar year ending the previous December 31.

Death of individual beneficiary. If an individual beneficiary dies, the beneficiary's share of the estate's distributable net income may be distributed or be considered distributed by the estate for its tax year that does not end with or within the last tax year of the beneficiary. In this case, the estate income that must be included in the gross income on the beneficiary's final return is based on the amounts distributed or considered distributed during the tax year of the estate in which his or her last tax year ended. However, for a cash basis beneficiary, the gross income of the last tax year includes only the amounts actually distributed before death. Income that must be distributed to the beneficiary but, in fact, is distributed to the beneficiary's estate after death is included in the gross income of the beneficiary's estate as income in respect of a decedent.

Termination of nonindividual beneficiary. If a beneficiary that is not an individual, for example a trust or a corporation, ceases to exist, the amount included in its gross income for its last tax year is determined as if the beneficiary were a deceased individual. However, income that must be distributed before termination, but which is actually distributed to the beneficiary's successor in interest, is included in the gross income of the nonindividual beneficiary for its last tax year.

Schedule K–1 (Form 1041). The personal representative for the estate must provide you with a copy of Schedule K–1 (Form 1041) or a substitute Schedule K–1. You should not file the form with your Form 1040, but should keep it for your personal records.

Each beneficiary (or nominee of a beneficiary) who receives a distribution from the estate for the tax year or to whom any item is allocated must receive a Schedule K–1 or substitute. The personal representative handling the estate must furnish the form to each beneficiary or nominee by the date on which the Form 1041 is filed.

Nominees. A person who holds an interest in an estate as a nominee for a beneficiary must provide the estate with the name and address of the beneficiary, and any other required information. The nominee must provide the beneficiary with the information received from the estate.

Penalty. A personal representative (or nominee) who fails to provide the correct information may be subject to a $50 penalty for each failure.

Consistent treatment of items. You must treat estate items the same way on your individual return as they are treated on the estate's income tax return. If your treatment is different from the estate's treatment, you must file Form 8082, *Notice of Inconsistent Treatment or Amended Return (Administrative Adjustment Request (AAR)),* with your return to identify the difference. If you do not file Form 8082 and the estate has filed a return, the IRS can immediately assess and collect any tax and penalties that result from adjusting the item to make it consistent with the estate's treatment.

Special Rules for Distributions

Some special rules apply for determining the deduction allowable to the estate for distributions to beneficiaries and the amount includible in the beneficiary's gross income.

Bequest

A bequest is the act of giving or leaving property to another through the last will and testament. Generally, any distribution of income (or property in kind) to a beneficiary is an allowable deduction to the estate and is includible in the beneficiary's gross income to the extent of the estate's distributable net income. However, it will not be an allowable deduction to the estate and will not be includible in the beneficiary's gross income if the distribution:

1) Is required by the terms of the will,
2) Is a gift or bequest of a ***specific sum of money or property,*** and
3) Is paid out in three or fewer installments under the terms of the will.

Specific sum of money or property. To meet this test, the amount of money or the identity of the specific property must be determinable under the decedent's will as of the date of death. To qualify as specific property, the property must be identifiable both as to its kind and as to its amount.

Example 1. Dave Rogers' will provided that his son, Ed, receive Dave's interest in the Rogers-Jones partnership. Dave's daughter, Marie, would receive a sum of money equal to the value of the partnership interest given to Ed. The bequest to Ed is a gift of a specific property ascertainable at the date of Dave Rogers' death. The bequest of a specific sum of money to Marie is determinable on the same date.

Example 2. Mike Jenkins' will provided that his widow, Helen, would receive money or property to be selected by the personal representative equal in value to half of his adjusted gross estate. The identity of the property and the money in the bequest are dependent on the personal representative's discretion and the payment of administration expenses and other charges, which are not determinable at the date of Mike's death. As a result, the provision is not a bequest of a specific sum of money or of specific property, and any distribution under that provision is a deduction for the estate and income to the beneficiary (to the extent of the estate's distributable net income). The fact that the bequest will be specific sometime before distribution is immaterial. It is not ascertainable by the terms of the will as of the date of death.

Distributions not treated as bequests. The following distributions are not bequests that meet all of the three tests listed earlier that allow a distribution to be excluded from the beneficiary's income and do not allow it as a deduction to the estate.

Paid only from income. An amount that can be paid only from current or prior income of the estate does not qualify even if it is specific in amount and there is no provision for installment payments.

An annuity. An annuity or a payment of money or of specific property in lieu of, or having the effect of, an annuity is not the payment of a specific property or sum of money.

Residuary estate. If the will provides for the payment of the balance or residue of the estate to a beneficiary of the estate after all expenses and other specific legacies or bequests, that residuary bequest is not a payment of a specific property or sum of money.

Gifts made in installments. Even if the gift or bequest is made in a lump sum or in three or fewer installments, it will not qualify as a specific property or sum of money if the will provides that the amount must be paid in more than three installments.

Conditional bequests. A bequest of a specific property or sum of money that may otherwise be excluded from the beneficiary's gross income will not lose the exclusion solely because the payment is subject to a condition.

Installment payments. Certain rules apply in determining whether a bequest of specific property or a sum of money has to be paid or credited to a beneficiary in more than three installments.

Personal items. Do not take into account bequests of articles for personal use, such as personal and household effects and automobiles.

Real property. Do not take into account specifically designated real property, the title to which passes under local law directly to the beneficiary.

Other property. All other bequests under the decedent's will for which no time of payment or crediting is specified and that are to be paid or credited in the ordinary course of administration of the estate are considered as required to be paid or credited in a single installment. Also, all bequests payable at any one specified time under the terms of the will are treated as a single installment.

A testamentary trust. In determining the number of installments that must be paid or credited to a beneficiary, the decedent's estate and a testamentary trust created by the decedent's will are treated as separate entities. Amounts paid or credited by the estate and by the trust are counted separately.

Denial of Double Deduction

A deduction cannot be claimed twice. If an amount is considered to have been distributed to a beneficiary of an estate in a preceding tax year, it cannot again be included in figuring the deduction for the year of the actual distribution.

Example. The will provides that the estate must distribute currently all of its income to a beneficiary. For administrative convenience, the personal representative did not make a distribution of a part of the income for the tax year until the first month of the next tax year. The amount must be deducted by the estate in the first tax year, and must be included in the gross income of the beneficiary in that year. This amount cannot be deducted again by the estate in the following year when it is paid to the beneficiary, nor must the beneficiary again include the amount in gross income in that year.

Charitable Contributions

The amount of a charitable contribution used as a deduction by the estate in determining taxable income cannot be claimed again as a deduction for a distribution to a beneficiary.

Termination of Estate

The termination of an estate generally is marked by the end of the period of administration and by the distribution of the assets to the beneficiaries under the terms of the will or under the laws of succession of the state if there is no will. These beneficiaries may or may not be the same persons as the beneficiaries of the estate's income.

Period of Administration

The period of administration is the time actually required by the personal representative to assemble all of the decedent's assets, pay all the expenses and obligations, and distribute the assets to the beneficiaries. This may be longer or shorter than the time provided by local law for the administration of estates.

Ends if all assets distributed. If all assets are distributed except for a reasonable amount set aside, in good faith, for the payment of unascertained or contingent liabilities and expenses (but not including a claim by a beneficiary, as a beneficiary) the estate will be considered terminated.

Ends if period unreasonably long. If settlement is prolonged unreasonably, the estate will be treated as terminated for federal income tax purposes. From that point on, the gross income, deductions, and credits of the estate are considered those of the person or persons succeeding to the property of the estate.

Transfer of Unused Deductions to Beneficiaries

If the estate has unused loss carryovers or excess deductions for its last tax year, they are allowed to those beneficiaries who succeed to the estate's property. See *Successor beneficiary,* later.

Unused loss carryovers. An unused net operating loss carryover or capital loss carryover existing upon termination of the estate is allowed to the beneficiaries succeeding to the property of the estate. That is, these deductions will be claimed on the beneficiary's tax return. This treatment occurs only if a carryover would have been allowed to the estate in a later tax year if the estate had not been terminated.

Both types of carryovers generally keep their same character for the beneficiary as they had for the estate. However, if the beneficiary of a capital loss carryover is a corporation, the corporation will treat the carryover as a short-term capital loss regardless of its status in the estate. The net operating loss carryover and the capital loss carryover are used in figuring the beneficiary's adjusted gross income and taxable income. The beneficiary may have to adjust any net operating loss carryover in figuring the alternative minimum tax.

The first tax year to which the loss is carried is the beneficiary's tax year in which the estate terminates. If the loss can be carried to more than one tax year, the estate's last tax year (whether or not a short tax year) and the beneficiary's first tax year to which the loss is carried each constitute a tax year for figuring the number of years to which a loss may be carried. A capital loss carryover from an estate to a corporate beneficiary will be treated as though it resulted from a loss incurred in the estate's last tax year (whether or not a short tax year), regardless of when the estate actually incurred the loss.

If the last tax year of the estate is the last tax year to which a net operating loss may be carried, see *No double deductions,* later. For a general discussion of net operating losses, get Publication 536. For a discussion of capital losses and capital loss carryovers, get Publication 550.

Excess deductions. If the deductions in the estate's last tax year (other than deductions for personal exemptions and charitable contributions) are more than gross income for that year, the beneficiaries succeeding to the estate's property can claim the excess as a deduction in figuring taxable income. To establish these deductions, a return must be filed for the estate along with a schedule showing the computation of each kind of deduction and the allocation of each to the beneficiaries.

An individual beneficiary must itemize deductions to claim these excess deductions. The deduction is claimed on Schedule A, Form 1040, as a miscellaneous itemized deduction subject to the 2%-of-adjusted-gross-income limit. The beneficiaries can claim the deduction only for the tax year in which or with which the estate terminates, whether the year of termination is a normal year or a short tax year.

No double deductions. A net operating loss deduction allowable to a successor beneficiary cannot be considered in figuring the excess deductions on termination. However, if the estate's last tax year is the last year in which a deduction for a net operating loss can be taken, the deduction, to the extent not absorbed in the last return of the estate, is treated as an excess deduction on termination. Any item of income or deduction, or any part thereof, that is taken into account in figuring a net operating loss or a capital loss carryover of the estate for its last tax year cannot be used again to figure the excess deduction on termination.

Successor beneficiary. A beneficiary entitled to an unused loss carryover or an excess deduction is the beneficiary who, upon the estate's termination, bears the burden of any loss for which a carryover is allowed or of any deductions more than gross income.

If decedent had no will. If the decedent had no will, the beneficiaries are those heirs or next of kin to whom the estate is distributed. If the estate is insolvent, the beneficiaries are those to whom the estate would have been distributed had it not been insolvent. If the decedent's spouse is entitled to a specified dollar amount of property before any distributions to other heirs and the estate is less than that amount, the spouse is the beneficiary to the extent of the deficiency.

If decedent had a will. If the decedent had a will, a beneficiary normally means the residuary beneficiaries (including residuary trusts). Those beneficiaries who receive a specific property or a specific amount of money ordinarily are not considered residuary beneficiaries, except to the extent the specific amount is not paid in full. Also, a beneficiary who is not strictly a residuary beneficiary, but whose devise or bequest is determined by the value of the estate as reduced by the loss or deduction, is entitled to the carryover or the deduction. For example, such a beneficiary would include:

1) A beneficiary of a fraction of the decedent's net estate after payment of debts, expenses, and specific bequests;
2) A nonresiduary beneficiary, when the estate is unable to satisfy the bequest in full; and
3) A surviving spouse receiving a fractional share of the estate in fee under a statutory right of election when the losses or deductions are taken into account in determining the share. However, such a beneficiary does not include a recipient of a dower or curtesy, or a beneficiary who receives any income from the estate from which the loss or excess deduction is carried over.

Allocation among beneficiaries. The total of the unused loss carryovers or the excess deductions on termination that may be deducted by the successor beneficiaries is to be divided according to the share of each in the burden of the loss or deduction.

Example. Under his father's will, Arthur is to receive $20,000. The remainder of the estate is to be divided equally between his brothers, Mark and Tom. After all expenses are paid, the estate has sufficient funds to pay Arthur only $15,000, with nothing to Mark and Tom. In the estate's last tax year there are excess deductions of $5,000 and $10,000 of unused loss carryovers. Since the total of the excess deductions and unused loss carryovers is $15,000 and Arthur is considered a successor beneficiary to the extent of $5,000, he is entitled to one-third of the unused loss carryover and one-third of the excess deductions. His brothers may divide the other two-thirds of the excess deductions and the unused loss carryovers between them.

Transfer of Credit for Estimated Tax Payments

When an estate terminates, the personal representative can choose to transfer to the beneficiaries the credit for all or part of the estate's estimated tax payments for the last tax year. To make this choice, the personal representative must complete Form 1041–T, *Allocation of Estimated Tax Payments to Beneficiaries,* and file it either separately or with the estate's final Form 1041. The Form 1041–T must be filed by the 65th day after the close of the estate's tax year.

The amount of estimated tax allocated to each beneficiary is treated as paid or credited to the beneficiary on the last day of the estate's final tax year and must be reported on line 14a, Schedule K–1 (Form 1041). If the estate terminated in 1997 this amount is treated as a payment of 1997 estimated tax made by the beneficiary on January 15, 1998.

Form 706

You must file Form 706, *United States Estate (and Generation-Skipping Transfer) Tax Return,* generally, if death occurred in 1997 and the gross estate is more than $600,000.

If you must file Form 706, it has to be done within 9 months after the date of the decedent's death unless you receive an extension of time to file. File this form with the Internal Revenue Service center listed in the form instructions.

Use Form 4768, *Application for Extension of Time To File a Return and/or Pay U.S. Estate (and Generation-Skipping Transfer) Taxes,* to apply for an extension of time. If you received an extension, attach a copy of it to Form 706.

Comprehensive Example

The following is an example of a typical situation. All figures on the filled-in forms have been rounded to the nearest whole dollar.

On April 9, 1997, your father, John R. Smith, died at the age of 62. He had not resided in a community property state. His will named you to serve as his executor (personal representative). Except for specific bequests to your mother, Mary, of your parents' home and your father's automobile and a bequest of $5,000 to his church, your father's will named your mother and his brother as beneficiaries.

One of the first things you should do, as soon as the court has approved your appointment as the executor, is to obtain an employer identification number for the estate. (See *Duties* under *Personal Representatives* earlier.) Next, you should notify the Internal Revenue Service center where you will file the tax returns of your father's estate that you have been appointed his executor. You should use Form 56.

Assets of the estate. Your father had the following assets when he died.

1) His checking account balance was $2,550, and his savings account balance was $53,650.
2) Your father inherited your parents' home from his parents on March 5, 1977. At that time it was worth $42,000, but was appraised at the time of your father's death to be worth $150,000. The home was free of existing debts (or mortgages) at the time of his death.
3) Your father owned 500 shares of ABC Company stock that had cost him $10.20 a share in 1981, but which had a mean selling price (midpoint between highest and lowest selling price) of $25 a share on the day he died. He also owned 500 shares of XYZ Company stock that had cost him $20 a share in 1986, but which had a mean selling price on the date of death of $62.
4) The appraiser valued your father's automobile at $6,300 and the household effects at $18,500.
5) Your father also owned coin and stamp collections. The face value of the coins in the collection was only $600, but the appraiser valued it at $2,800. The stamp collection was valued at $3,500.
6) Your father's employer sent a check to your mother for $11,082 ($12,000 minus $918 for social security and Medicare taxes), representing unpaid salary and payment for accrued vacation time. The statement that came with the check indicated that no amount was withheld for income tax. Since the check was made out to the estate, your mother gave you the check.
7) The Easy Life Insurance Company had given a check for $275,000 to your mother as the beneficiary named in the life insurance policy on his life.
8) Your father was the owner of several Series EE U.S. Savings Bonds on which he named your mother as co-owner. Your father purchased the bonds during the past several years. The cost of these bonds totaled $2,500. After referring to the appropriate table of redemption values (see *U.S. Savings Bonds acquired from decedent,* earlier in this publication), you determine that interest of $840 had accrued on the bonds at the date of your father's death. You must include the redemption value of these bonds at date of death, $3,340, in your father's gross estate.
9) On July 1, 1980, your parents purchased a house for $90,000. They have held the property for rental purposes continuously since its purchase. Your mother contributed one-third of the purchase, or $30,000 (from an inheritance), and your father contributed $60,000. They owned the property, however, as joint tenants with right of survivorship. An appraiser valued the property at $110,000. You include $55,000, one-half of the value, in your father's gross estate because your parents owned the property as joint

tenants with right of survivorship and they were the only joint tenants.

Your mother also gave you a Form W–2, *Wage and Tax Statement,* that your father's employer had sent. In examining it, you discover that your father had been paid $9,000 in salary between January 1, 1997, and April 9, 1997, (the date he died). The Form W–2 showed $9,000 in box 1 and $21,000 ($9,000 + $12,000) in boxes 3 and 5. The Form W–2 indicated $2,305 as federal income tax withheld in box 2. The estate received a Form 1099–MISC from the employer showing $12,000 in box 3. The estate received a Form 1099–INT for your father showing he was paid $1,900 interest on his savings account in 1997 before he died.

Final Return for Decedent

Checking the papers in your father's files, you determine that the $9,000 paid to him by his employer (as shown on the Form W–2), rental income, and interest are the only items of income he received between January 1 and the date of his death. You will have to file an income tax return for him for the period during which he lived. (You determine that he timely filed his 1996 income tax return before he died.) The final return is not due until April 15, 1998, the same date it would have been due had your father lived during all of 1997.

Since the check representing unpaid salary and earned but unused vacation time was not paid to your father before he died, the $12,000 is not reported as income on his final return. It is reported on the income tax return for the estate (Form 1041) for 1997. The only taxable income to be reported for your father will be the $9,000 salary (as shown on the Form W–2), the $1,900 interest, and his portion of the rental income that he received in 1997.

Your father was a cash basis taxpayer and did not report the interest accrued on the Series EE U.S. Savings Bonds on prior tax returns that he filed jointly with your mother. As the personal representative of your father's estate, you choose to report the interest earned on these bonds before your father's death ($840) on the final income tax return.

The rental property was leased the entire year of 1997 for $700 per month. Under local law, your parents (as joint tenants) each had a half interest in the income from the property. Your father's will, however, stipulates that the entire rental income is to be paid directly to your mother. None of the rental income will be reported on the income tax return for the estate. Instead, your mother will report all the rental income and expenses on Form 1040. Checking the records and prior tax returns of your parents, you find that they previously elected straight-line depreciation for the rental house with a 25–year life. They allocated $15,000 of the cost to the land (which is never depreciable) and $75,000 to the rental house. Salvage value was disregarded for the depreciation computation. Before 1997, $49,500 had been allowed as depreciation.

Deductions. During the year, you received a bill from the hospital for $615 and bills from your father's doctors totaling $475. You paid these bills as they were presented. In addition, you find other bills from his doctors totaling $185 that your father paid in 1997, and receipts for prescribed drugs he purchased totaling $36. The funeral home presented you a bill for $6,890 for the expenses of your father's funeral, which you paid.

Because the medical expenses you paid from the estate's funds ($475 and $615) were for your father's care and were paid within 1 year after his death, and because they will not be used to figure the taxable estate, you can treat them as having been paid by your father when he received the medical services. See *Funeral and Medical Expenses* under *Income Tax Return of an Estate–Form 1041* and its discussion, *Exemption and Deductions,* earlier. However, you cannot deduct the funeral expenses either on your father's final return or from the estate's income. They are deductible only on the federal estate tax return (Form 706) as explained under *Funeral and Medical Expenses.*

In addition, after going over other receipts and canceled checks for the tax year with your mother, you determine that the following items are deductible on your parents' 1997 income tax return.

Health insurance	$1,250
State income tax paid	791
Real estate tax on home	1,100
Contributions to church	3,800

Rental expenses included taxes of $700 and interest of $410 on the property; in addition, insurance premiums of $260 and painting and repairs for $350 were paid. These rental expenses totaled $1,720 for the whole year.

Because your mother and father owned the property as joint tenants with right of survivorship and they were the only joint tenants, her basis in this property upon your father's death is $74,875. This is found by adding the $55,000 value of the half interest included in your father's gross estate to your mother's $45,000 share of the cost basis, and subtracting your mother's $25,125 share of depreciation (including 1997 depreciation for the period before your father's death), as explained next.

For 1997, you must make the following computations to figure the depreciation deduction:

1) For the period before your father's death, depreciate the property using the same method and the same basis and life used by your parents in previous years. The amount deductible for one-fourth of the year is $750. (This brings the total depreciation to $50,250 ($49,500 + $750) at the time of your father's death.

2) For the period after your father's death, you must make two computations.

   a) Your mother's cost basis ($45,000) minus one-half of the amount allocated to the land ($7,500) is her depreciable basis ($37,500) for half of the property. She continues to use the same life and depreciation method as was originally used for the property. The amount deductible for three-fourths of the year is $1,125.

   b) The other half of the property must be depreciated using a depreciation method that is acceptable for property placed in service in 1997. You elect to use the alternative depreciation system (straight-line method) with the mid-month convention. The value included in the estate ($55,000) less the value allocable to the land ($10,000) is the depreciable basis ($45,000) for this half of the property. The amount deductible for this half of the property is $797 ($45,000 .01771). See chapter 3 and Table A–13 in Publication 946.

Show the total of the amounts in (1) and (2)(a), above, on line 19 of Form 4562, *Depreciation and Amortization.* Show the amount in (2)(b) on line 16c. The total depreciation deduction allowed for the year is $2,672.

The use of certain types of accelerated depreciation would require you to fill out a Form 6251, Alternative Minimum Tax—Individuals. Use of the straight-line method does not require this.

Filing status. After December 31, 1997, when your mother determines the amount of her income, you and your mother must decide whether you will file a joint return or separate returns for your parents for 1997. Since your mother has no income in 1997 other than the rental income, it appears to be to her advantage to file a joint return.

Tax computation. The illustrations of Form 1040 and related schedules appear at the end of this publication. These illustrations are based on information in this example. The tax refund is $1,799. The computation is as follows:

Income:		
Salary (per Form W–2)	$9,000	
Interest income	2,740	
Net rental income	4,008	
Adjusted Gross Income		$15,748
Minus: Itemized deductions		7,071
Balance		$8,677
Minus: Exemptions (2)		5,300
Taxable Income		$3,377
Income tax from Tax Table		$506
Minus: Tax withheld		2,305
Refund of Taxes		$1,799

Income Tax Return of an Estate—Form 1041

The illustrations of Form 1041 and the related schedules appear at the end of this publication. These illustrations are based on the information that follows.

Having determined the tax liability for your father's final return, you now figure the estate's taxable income. You decide to use the calendar year and the cash method of accounting to report the estate's income. This return also is due by April 15, 1998.

In addition to the amount you received from your father's employer for unpaid salary and for vacation pay ($12,000) entered on line 8 (Form 1041), you received a dividend check from the XYZ Company on June 16, 1997. The check was for $750 and you enter it on line 2 (Form 1041). The estate received a Form 1099–INT showing $2,250 interest paid by the bank on the savings account in 1997 after your father died. Show this amount on line 1 (Form 1041).

In September, a local coin collector offered you $3,000 for your father's coin collection, and since your mother was not interested in keeping the collection, you accepted the offer and sold him the collection on September 22, 1997, receiving his certified check for $3,000.

The estate has a gain from the sale of the collection. You will have to report the sale on

Schedule D (Form 1041) when you file the income tax return of the estate. The estate has a capital gain of $200 from the sale of the coins. The gain is the excess of the sale price, $3,000, over the value of the collection at the date of your father's death, $2,800. See *Gain (or loss) from sale of property* under *Income Tax Return of an Estate–Form 1041* and its discussion, *Income To Include,* earlier.

Deductions. In November 1997, you received a bill for the real estate taxes on the home. The bill was for $2,250, which you paid. Include real estate taxes on line 11 (Form 1041). (Real estate tax on the rental property was $700; this amount, however, is reflected on Schedule E (Form 1040).)

You paid $325 for attorney's fees in connection with administration of the estate. This is an expense of administration and is deducted on line 14 (Form 1041). You must, however, file with the return a statement in duplicate that such expense has not been claimed as a deduction from the gross estate for figuring the federal estate tax on Form 706, and that all rights to claim that deduction are waived.

Distributions. Under the terms of the will, you made a distribution of $2,000 to your father's brother, James. The distribution was made from current income of the estate.

The income distribution deduction ($2,000) is figured on Schedule B of Form 1041 and deducted on line 18 (Form 1041).

The distribution of $2,000 must be allocated and reported on Schedule K–1 (Form 1041) as follows:

Step 1
Allocation of Income and Deductions:

Type of Income	Amount	Deductions	Balance of Distributable Net Income
Interest (15%)	$ 2,250	(386)	$ 1,864
Dividends (5%)	750	(129)	621
Income in Respect of Decedent	12,000	(2,060)	9,940
Total	$15,000	(2,575)	$12,425

Step 2
Allocation of Distribution to be reported on Schedule K–1 (Form 1041) for James:

Interest—			
$1,864	2,000/12,425 =	$ 300	line 1
Dividends—			
$621	2,000/12,425 =	100	line 2
Other Income—			
$9,940	2,000/12,425 =	1,600	line 5a
Total Distribution		$2,000	

Since the estate took an income distribution deduction, you must prepare Schedule I (Form 1041), *Alternative Minimum Tax,* regardless of whether the estate is liable for the alternative minimum tax.

The other distribution you made out of the assets of the estate in 1997 was the transfer of the automobile to your mother on July 1. Because this is included in the bequest of property, it is not taken into account in computing the distributions of income to the beneficiary. The life insurance proceeds of $275,000 paid directly to your mother by the insurance company are treated as a specific sum of money transferred to your mother under the terms of the will.

The taxable income of the estate for 1997 is $10,025, figured as follows:

Gross income:		
Income in respect of a decedent		$12,000
Dividends		750
Interest		2,250
Capital gain		200
		$15,200
Minus: Deductions & Income Distribution		
Real estate taxes	$2,250	
Attorney's fee	325	
Exemption	600	
Distribution	2,000	5,175
Taxable income		$10,025

Since the estate had a net capital gain and taxable income, you use Part V of Schedule D (Form 1041) to figure the tax, $3,026, for 1997.

1998 income tax return for estate. On January 6, 1998, you receive a dividend check from the XYZ Company for $500. You also have interest posted to the savings account in January totaling $350. On January 26, 1998, you make a final accounting to the court and obtain permission to close the estate. In the accounting you list $1,650 as the balance of the expense of administering the estate.

You advise the court that you plan to pay $5,000 to Hometown Church, under the provision of the will, and that you will distribute the balance of the property to your mother, Mary Smith, the remaining beneficiary.

Gross income. After making the distributions already described, you can wind up the affairs of the estate. Because the gross income of the estate for 1998 is more than $600, you must file an income tax return, Form 1041, for 1998 (not shown). The estate's gross income for 1998 is $850 (dividends $500 and interest $350).

Deductions. After making the following computations, you determine that none of the distributions made to your mother must be included in her taxable income for 1998.

Gross Income for 1998:	
Dividends	$500
Interest	350
	$850
Less deductions:	
Administration expense	$1,650
Loss	($800)

Note that because the contribution of $5,000 to Hometown Church was not required under the terms of the will to be paid out of the gross income of the estate, it is not deductible and was not included in the computation.

Because the estate had no distributable net income in 1998, none of the distributions made to your mother has to be included in her gross income. Furthermore, because the estate in the year of termination had deductions in excess of its gross income, the excess of $800 will be allowed as a miscellaneous itemized deduction subject to the 2%-of-adjusted-gross-income limit to your mother on her individual return for the year 1998, if she is otherwise eligible to itemize deductions.

Termination of estate. You have made the final distribution of the assets of the estate and you are now ready to terminate the estate. You must notify the IRS, in writing, that the estate has been terminated and that all of the assets have been distributed to the beneficiaries. Form 56, mentioned earlier, can be used for this purpose. Be sure to report the termination to the IRS office where you filed Form 56 and to include the employer identification number on this notification.

How To Get More Information

You can get help from the IRS in several ways.

Free publications and forms. To order free publications and forms, call 1–800–TAX–FORM (1–800–829–3676). You can also write to the IRS Forms Distribution Center nearest you. Check your income tax package for the address. Your local library or post office also may have the items you need.

For a list of free tax publications, order Publication 910, *Guide to Free Tax Services.* It also contains an index of tax topics and related publications and describes other free tax information services available from IRS, including tax education and assistance programs.

If you have access to a personal computer and modem, you also can get many forms and publications electronically. See your income tax package for details.

Tax questions. You can call the IRS with your tax questions. Check your income tax package or telephone book for the local number, or you can call 1–800–829–1040.

TTY/TDD equipment. If you have access to TTY/TDD equipment, you can call 1–800–829–4059 to ask tax questions or to order forms and publications. See your income tax package for the hours of operation.

Evaluating the quality of our telephone services. To ensure that IRS representatives give accurate, courteous, and professional answers, we evaluate the quality of our "800 number" telephone services in several ways.

- A second IRS representative sometimes monitors live telephone calls. That person only evaluates the IRS assistor and does not keep a record of any taxpayer's name or tax identification number.
- We sometimes record telephone calls to evaluate IRS assistors objectively. We hold these recordings no longer than one week and use them only to measure the quality of assistance.
- We value our customers' opinions. Throughout this year, we will be surveying our customers for their opinions on our service.

DECEASED John R. Smith -- April 9, 1997

Form **1040** Department of the Treasury—Internal Revenue Service
U.S. Individual Income Tax Return 1997 IRS Use Only—Do not write or staple in this space.

For the year Jan. 1–Dec. 31, 1997, or other tax year beginning , 1997, ending , 19 OMB No. 1545-0074

Label (See instructions on page 10.) **Use the IRS label.** Otherwise, please print or type.

LABEL HERE

Your first name and initial	Last name	Your social security number
John R.	Smith	234 : 00 : 7890
If a joint return, spouse's first name and initial	Last name	Spouse's social security number
Mary L.	Smith	567 : 00 : 0123
Home address (number and street). If you have a P.O. box, see page 10.	Apt. no.	
6406 Mayflower St.		
City, town or post office, state, and ZIP code. If you have a foreign address, see page 10.		
Juneville, ME 00000		

For help in finding line instructions, see pages 2 and 3 in the booklet.

Presidential Election Campaign (See page 10.)

	Yes	No
Do you want $3 to go to this fund?	✓	
If a joint return, does your spouse want $3 to go to this fund?	✓	

Note: *Checking "Yes" will not change your tax or reduce your refund.*

Filing Status

Check only one box.

1 [ ] Single
2 [✓] Married filing joint return (even if only one had income)
3 [ ] Married filing separate return. Enter spouse's social security no. above and full name here. ▶
4 [ ] Head of household (with qualifying person). (See page 10.) If the qualifying person is a child but not your dependent, enter this child's name here. ▶
5 [ ] Qualifying widow(er) with dependent child (year spouse died ▶ 19). (See page 10.)

Exemptions

6a [✓] **Yourself.** If your parent (or someone else) can claim you as a dependent on his or her tax return, **do not** check box 6a.
b [✓] **Spouse**

No. of boxes checked on 6a and 6b: 2

c **Dependents:**

(1) First name Last name	(2) Dependent's social security number	(3) Dependent's relationship to you	(4) No. of months lived in your home in 1997

If more than six dependents, see page 10.

No. of your children on 6c who:
- **lived with you**
- **did not live with you due to divorce or separation (see page 11)**

Dependents on 6c not entered above

Add numbers entered on lines above ▶ 2

d Total number of exemptions claimed

Income

Attach Copy B of your Forms W-2, W-2G, and 1099-R here.

If you did not get a W-2, see page 12.

Enclose but do not attach any payment. Also, please use **Form 1040-V.**

Line	Description		Amount
7	Wages, salaries, tips, etc. Attach Form(s) W-2	7	9,000
8a	**Taxable** interest. Attach Schedule B if required	8a	2,740
b	**Tax-exempt** interest. DO NOT include on line 8a [8b]		
9	Dividends. Attach Schedule B if required	9	
10	Taxable refunds, credits, or offsets of state and local income taxes (see page 12)	10	
11	Alimony received	11	
12	Business income or (loss). Attach Schedule C or C-EZ	12	
13	Capital gain or (loss). Attach Schedule D	13	
14	Other gains or (losses). Attach Form 4797	14	
15a	Total IRA distributions [15a] b Taxable amount (see page 13)	15b	
16a	Total pensions and annuities [16a] b Taxable amount (see page 13)	16b	
17	Rental real estate, royalties, partnerships, S corporations, trusts, etc. Attach Schedule E	17	4,008
18	Farm income or (loss). Attach Schedule F	18	
19	Unemployment compensation	19	
20a	Social security benefits [20a] b Taxable amount (see page 14)	20b	
21	Other income. List type and amount—see page 15	21	
22	Add the amounts in the far right column for lines 7 through 21. This is your **total income** ▶	22	15,748

Adjusted Gross Income

If line 32 is under $29,290 (under $9,770 if a child did not live with you), see EIC inst. on page 21.

Line	Description		Amount		Amount
23	IRA deduction (see page 16)	23			
24	Medical savings account deduction. Attach Form 8853	24			
25	Moving expenses. Attach Form 3903 or 3903-F	25			
26	One-half of self-employment tax. Attach Schedule SE	26			
27	Self-employed health insurance deduction (see page 17)	27			
28	Keogh and self-employed SEP and SIMPLE plans	28			
29	Penalty on early withdrawal of savings	29			
30a	Alimony paid b Recipient's SSN ▶	30a			
31	Add lines 23 through 30a			31	
32	Subtract line 31 from line 22. This is your **adjusted gross income** ▶			32	15,748

For Privacy Act and Paperwork Reduction Act Notice, see page 38. Cat. No. 11320B Form **1040** (1997)

Page 24

Form 1040 (1997) Page **2**

Tax Computation	33	Amount from line 32 (adjusted gross income)		33	15,748
	34a	Check if: ☐ **You** were 65 or older, ☐ Blind; ☐ **Spouse** was 65 or older, ☐ Blind. Add the number of boxes checked above and enter the total here ▶ 34a			
	b	If you are married filing separately and your spouse itemizes deductions or you were a dual-status alien, see page 18 and check here ▶ 34b ☐			
	35	Enter the **larger** of your: **Itemized deductions** from Schedule A, line 28, **OR** **Standard deduction** shown below for your filing status. **But** see page 18 if you checked any box on line 34a or 34b **or** someone can claim you as a dependent. • Single—$4,150 • Married filing jointly or Qualifying widow(er)—$6,900 • Head of household—$6,050 • Married filing separately—$3,450		35	7,071
If you want the IRS to figure your tax, see page 18.	36	Subtract line 35 from line 33		36	8,677
	37	If line 33 is $90,900 or less, multiply $2,650 by the total number of exemptions claimed on line 6d. If line 33 is over $90,900, see the worksheet on page 19 for the amount to enter		37	5,300
	38	**Taxable income.** Subtract line 37 from line 36. If line 37 is more than line 36, enter -0-		38	3,377
	39	**Tax.** See page 19. Check if any tax from **a** ☐ Form(s) 8814 **b** ☐ Form 4972 ▶		39	506
Credits	40	Credit for child and dependent care expenses. Attach Form 2441	40		
	41	Credit for the elderly or the disabled. Attach Schedule R	41		
	42	Adoption credit. Attach Form 8839	42		
	43	Foreign tax credit. Attach Form 1116	43		
	44	Other. Check if from **a** ☐ Form 3800 **b** ☐ Form 8396 **c** ☐ Form 8801 **d** ☐ Form (specify) ______	44		
	45	Add lines 40 through 44		45	
	46	Subtract line 45 from line 39. If line 45 is more than line 39, enter -0- ▶		46	506
Other Taxes	47	Self-employment tax. Attach Schedule SE		47	
	48	Alternative minimum tax. Attach Form 6251		48	
	49	Social security and Medicare tax on tip income not reported to employer. Attach Form 4137		49	
	50	Tax on qualified retirement plans (including IRAs) and MSAs. Attach Form 5329 if required		50	
	51	Advance earned income credit payments from Form(s) W-2		51	
	52	Household employment taxes. Attach Schedule H		52	
	53	Add lines 46 through 52. This is your **total tax** ▶		53	506
Payments	54	Federal income tax withheld from Forms W-2 and 1099	54 2,305		
	55	1997 estimated tax payments and amount applied from 1996 return	55		
	56a	**Earned income credit.** Attach Schedule EIC if you have a qualifying child **b** Nontaxable earned income: amount ▶ ______ and type ▶ ______	56a		
Attach Forms W-2, W-2G, and 1099-R on the front.	57	Amount paid with Form 4868 (request for extension)	57		
	58	Excess social security and RRTA tax withheld (see page 27)	58		
	59	Other payments. Check if from **a** ☐ Form 2439 **b** ☐ Form 4136	59		
	60	Add lines 54, 55, 56a, 57, 58, and 59. These are your **total payments** ▶		60	2,305
Refund	61	If line 60 is more than line 53, subtract line 53 from line 60. This is the amount you **OVERPAID**		61	1,799
Have it directly deposited! See page 27 and fill in 62b, 62c, and 62d.	62a	Amount of line 61 you want **REFUNDED TO YOU** ▶		62a	1,799
	▶ b	Routing number ______ ▶ **c** Type: ☐ Checking ☐ Savings			
	▶ d	Account number ______			
	63	Amount of line 61 you want **APPLIED TO YOUR 1998 ESTIMATED TAX** ▶	63		
Amount You Owe	64	If line 53 is more than line 60, subtract line 60 from line 53. This is the **AMOUNT YOU OWE.** For details on how to pay, see page 27 ▶		64	
	65	Estimated tax penalty. Also include on line 64	65		

Sign Here

Keep a copy of this return for your records.

Under penalties of perjury, I declare that I have examined this return and accompanying schedules and statements, and to the best of my knowledge and belief, they are true, correct, and complete. Declaration of preparer (other than taxpayer) is based on all information of which preparer has any knowledge.

Your signature	Date	Your occupation
Charles R Smith, Executor	3-25-98	
Spouse's signature. If a joint return, BOTH must sign.	Date	Spouse's occupation
Mary L. Smith	3-25-98	Homemaker

Paid Preparer's Use Only

Preparer's signature ▶	Date	Check if self-employed ☐	Preparer's social security no.
Firm's name (or yours if self-employed) and address ▶			EIN
			ZIP code

Printed on recycled paper

Page 25

SCHEDULES A&B (Form 1040)

Department of the Treasury
Internal Revenue Service

Schedule A—Itemized Deductions

(Schedule B is on back)

▶ Attach to Form 1040. ▶ See Instructions for Schedules A and B (Form 1040).

OMB No. 1545-0074

1997

Attachment Sequence No. **07**

Name(s) shown on Form 1040: John R. (Deceased) & Mary L. Smith

Your social security number: 234 : 00 : 7890

Section	Line	Description	Box	Amount	Line	Total
Medical and Dental Expenses		**Caution:** *Do not include expenses reimbursed or paid by others.*				
	1	Medical and dental expenses (see page A-1)	1	2,561		
	2	Enter amount from Form 1040, line 33 [2] 15,748				
	3	Multiply line 2 above by 7.5% (.075)	3	1,181		
	4	Subtract line 3 from line 1. If line 3 is more than line 1, enter -0-			4	1,380
Taxes You Paid (See page A-2.)	5	State and local income taxes	5	791		
	6	Real estate taxes (see page A-2)	6	1,100		
	7	Personal property taxes	7			
	8	Other taxes. List type and amount ▶	8			
	9	Add lines 5 through 8			9	1,891
Interest You Paid (See page A-2.)	10	Home mortgage interest and points reported to you on Form 1098	10			
	11	Home mortgage interest not reported to you on Form 1098. If paid to the person from whom you bought the home, see page A-3 and show that person's name, identifying no., and address ▶	11			
Note: Personal interest is not deductible.	12	**Points not reported to you on Form 1098. See page A-3 for special rules**	12			
	13	Investment interest. Attach Form 4952 if required. (See page A-3.)	13			
	14	Add lines 10 through 13			14	
Gifts to Charity If you made a gift and got a benefit for it, see page A-3.	15	Gifts by cash or check. If you made any gift of $250 or more, see page A-3	15	3,800		
	16	Other than by cash or check. If any gift of $250 or more, see page A-3. You **MUST** attach Form 8283 if over $500	16			
	17	Carryover from prior year	17			
	18	Add lines 15 through 17			18	3,800
Casualty and Theft Losses	19	Casualty or theft loss(es). Attach Form 4684. (See page A-4.)			19	
Job Expenses and Most Other Miscellaneous Deductions	20	Unreimbursed employee expenses—job travel, union dues, job education, etc. You **MUST** attach Form 2106 or 2106-EZ if required. (See page A-4.) ▶	20			
	21	Tax preparation fees	21			
(See page A-5 for expenses to deduct here.)	22	Other expenses—investment, safe deposit box, etc. List type and amount ▶	22			
	23	Add lines 20 through 22	23			
	24	Enter amount from Form 1040, line 33 [24]				
	25	Multiply line 24 above by 2% (.02)	25			
	26	Subtract line 25 from line 23. If line 25 is more than line 23, enter -0-			26	
Other Miscellaneous Deductions	27	Other—from list on page A-5. List type and amount ▶			27	
Total Itemized Deductions	28	Is Form 1040, line 33, over $121,200 (over $60,600 if married filing separately)? **NO.** Your deduction is not limited. Add the amounts in the far right column for lines 4 through 27. Also, enter on Form 1040, line 35, the **larger** of this amount or your standard deduction. **YES.** Your deduction may be limited. See page A-5 for the amount to enter. ▶			28	7,071

For Paperwork Reduction Act Notice, see Form 1040 instructions. Cat. No. 11330X **Schedule A (Form 1040) 1997**

Page 26

Schedules A&B (Form 1040) 1997 OMB No. 1545-0074 Page **2**

Name(s) shown on Form 1040. Do not enter name and social security number if shown on other side. | **Your social security number**

Schedule B—Interest and Dividend Income

Attachment Sequence No. **08**

Part I Interest Income

(See pages 12 and B-1.)

Note: *If you had over $400 in taxable interest income, you must also complete Part III.*

Note: If you received a Form 1099-INT, Form 1099-OID, or substitute statement from a brokerage firm, list the firm's name as the payer and enter the total interest shown on that form.

			Amount
1	List name of payer. If any interest is from a seller-financed mortgage and the buyer used the property as a personal residence, see page B-1 and list this interest first. Also, show that buyer's social security number and address ▶	1	
	First S&L of Juneville		1,900
	Series EE U.S. Savings Bonds -- Interest Includible Before Decedent's Death		840
2	Add the amounts on line 1	2	2,740
3	Excludable interest on series EE U.S. savings bonds issued after 1989 from Form 8815, line 14. You MUST attach Form 8815 to Form 1040	3	-0-
4	Subtract line 3 from line 2. Enter the result here and on Form 1040, line 8a ▶	4	2,740

Part II Dividend Income

(See pages 12 and B-1.)

Note: *If you had over $400 in gross dividends and/or other distributions on stock, you must also complete Part III.*

Note: If you received a Form 1099-DIV or substitute statement from a brokerage firm, list the firm's name as the payer and enter the total dividends shown on that form.

			Amount
5	List name of payer. Include gross dividends and/or other distributions on stock here. Any capital gain distributions and nontaxable distributions will be deducted on lines 7 and 8 ▶	5	
6	Add the amounts on line 5	6	
7	Capital gain distributions. Enter here and on Schedule D — 7		
8	Nontaxable distributions. (See the inst. for Form 1040, line 9.) — 8		
9	Add lines 7 and 8	9	
10	Subtract line 9 from line 6. Enter the result here and on Form 1040, line 9 ▶	10	

Part III Foreign Accounts and Trusts

(See page B-2.)

	You must complete this part if you **(a)** had over $400 of interest or dividends; **(b)** had a foreign account; or **(c)** received a distribution from, or were a grantor of, or a transferor to, a foreign trust.	Yes	No
11a	At any time during 1997, did you have an interest in or a signature or other authority over a financial account in a foreign country, such as a bank account, securities account, or other financial account? See page B-2 for exceptions and filing requirements for Form TD F 90-22.1		✓
b	If "Yes," enter the name of the foreign country ▶		
12	During 1997, did you receive a distribution from, or were you the grantor of, or transferor to, a foreign trust? If "Yes," you may have to file Form 3520 or 926. See page B-2		✓

For Paperwork Reduction Act Notice, see Form 1040 instructions. *Printed on recycled paper* **Schedule B (Form 1040) 1997**

Page 27

SCHEDULE E (Form 1040)
Department of the Treasury
Internal Revenue Service

Supplemental Income and Loss

(From rental real estate, royalties, partnerships, S corporations, estates, trusts, REMICs, etc.)

► **Attach to Form 1040 or Form 1041.** ► **See Instructions for Schedule E (Form 1040).**

OMB No. 1545-0074
1997
Attachment Sequence No. **13**

Name(s) shown on return: John R. (Deceased) & Mary L. Smith

Your social security number: 234 : 00 : 7890

Part I **Income or Loss From Rental Real Estate and Royalties** **Note:** *Report income and expenses from your business of renting personal property on* ***Schedule C*** *or* ***C-EZ*** *(see page E-1). Report farm rental income or loss from* ***Form 4835*** *on page 2, line 39.*

	1 Show the kind and location of each **rental real estate property:**
A	House, 137 Main Street, Juneville, ME 00000
B	
C	

2 For each rental real estate property listed on line 1, did you or your family use it during the tax year for personal purposes for more than the greater of:
- 14 days, **or**
- 10% of the total days rented at fair rental value?

(See page E-1.)

	Yes	No
A		√
B		
C		

Income:		Properties A	Properties B	Properties C		Totals (Add columns A, B, and C.)
3 Rents received	3	8,400			3	
4 Royalties received	4				4	
Expenses:						
5 Advertising	5					
6 Auto and travel (see page E-2).	6					
7 Cleaning and maintenance	7					
8 Commissions	8					
9 Insurance	9	260				
10 Legal and other professional fees	10					
11 Management fees	11					
12 Mortgage interest paid to banks, etc. (see page E-2)	12	410			12	
13 Other interest	13					
14 Repairs	14	350				
15 Supplies	15					
16 Taxes	16	700				
17 Utilities	17					
18 Other (list) ►	18					
19 Add lines 5 through 18	19	1,720			19	
20 Depreciation expense or depletion (see page E-2)	20	2,672			20	
21 Total expenses. Add lines 19 and 20	21	4,392				
22 Income or (loss) from rental real estate or royalty properties. Subtract line 21 from line 3 (rents) or line 4 (royalties). If the result is a (loss), see page E-3 to find out if you must file **Form 6198**	22	4,008				
23 Deductible rental real estate loss. **Caution:** *Your rental real estate loss on line 22 may be limited. See page E-3 to find out if you must file* ***Form 8582****. Real estate professionals must complete line 42 on page 2*	23	( )	( )	( )		

24 **Income.** Add positive amounts shown on line 22. **Do not** include any losses	24	4,008
25 **Losses.** Add royalty losses from line 22 and rental real estate losses from line 23. Enter total losses here	25	( )
26 Total rental real estate and royalty income or (loss). Combine lines 24 and 25. Enter the result here. If Parts II, III, IV, and line 39 on page 2 do not apply to you, also enter this amount on Form 1040, line 17. Otherwise, include this amount in the total on line 40 on page 2	26	4,008

For Paperwork Reduction Act Notice, see Form 1040 instructions. Cat. No. 11344L **Schedule E (Form 1040) 1997**

Page 28

Form **4562** | **Depreciation and Amortization** | OMB No. 1545-0172

Department of the Treasury
Internal Revenue Service

(Including Information on Listed Property)

▶ See separate instructions. ▶ Attach this form to your return.

1997
Attachment Sequence No. **67**

Name(s) shown on return	Business or activity to which this form relates	Identifying number
John R. (Deceased) & Mary L. Smith		234-00-7890

Part I — Election To Expense Certain Tangible Property (Section 179) (Note: *If you have any "listed property," complete Part V before you complete Part I.*)

1	Maximum dollar limitation. If an enterprise zone business, see page 2 of the instructions	1	$18,000
2	Total cost of section 179 property placed in service. See page 2 of the instructions	2	
3	Threshold cost of section 179 property before reduction in limitation	3	$200,000
4	Reduction in limitation. Subtract line 3 from line 2. If zero or less, enter -0-	4	
5	Dollar limitation for tax year. Subtract line 4 from line 1. If zero or less, enter -0-. If married filing separately, see page 2 of the instructions	5	

	(a) Description of property	(b) Cost (business use only)	(c) Elected cost
6			

7	Listed property. Enter amount from line 27	7	
8	Total elected cost of section 179 property. Add amounts in column (c), lines 6 and 7	8	
9	Tentative deduction. Enter the smaller of line 5 or line 8	9	
10	Carryover of disallowed deduction from 1996. See page 3 of the instructions	10	
11	Business income limitation. Enter the smaller of business income (not less than zero) or line 5 (see instructions)	11	
12	Section 179 expense deduction. Add lines 9 and 10, but do not enter more than line 11	12	
13	Carryover of disallowed deduction to 1998. Add lines 9 and 10, less line 12 ▶	13	

Note: *Do not use Part II or Part III below for listed property (automobiles, certain other vehicles, cellular telephones, certain computers, or property used for entertainment, recreation, or amusement). Instead, use Part V for listed property.*

Part II — MACRS Depreciation For Assets Placed in Service ONLY During Your 1997 Tax Year (Do Not Include Listed Property.)

Section A—General Asset Account Election

14 If you are making the election under section 168(i)(4) to group any assets placed in service during the tax year into one or more general asset accounts, check this box. See page 3 of the instructions ▶ ☐

Section B—General Depreciation System (GDS) (See page 3 of the instructions.)

(a) Classification of property	(b) Month and year placed in service	(c) Basis for depreciation (business/investment use only—see instructions)	(d) Recovery period	(e) Convention	(f) Method	(g) Depreciation deduction
15a 3-year property						
b 5-year property						
c 7-year property						
d 10-year property						
e 15-year property						
f 20-year property						
g 25-year property			25 yrs.		S/L	
h Residential rental property			27.5 yrs.	MM	S/L	
			27.5 yrs.	MM	S/L	
i Nonresidential real property			39 yrs.	MM	S/L	
				MM	S/L	

Section C—Alternative Depreciation System (ADS) (See page 6 of the instructions.)

16a Class life					S/L	
b 12-year			12 yrs.		S/L	
c 40-year	4-97	45,000	40 yrs.	MM	S/L	797

Part III — Other Depreciation (Do Not Include Listed Property.) (See page 6 of the instructions.)

17	GDS and ADS deductions for assets placed in service in tax years beginning before 1997	17	
18	Property subject to section 168(f)(1) election	18	
19	ACRS and other depreciation	19	1,875

Part IV — Summary (See page 7 of the instructions.)

20	Listed property. Enter amount from line 26	20	
21	**Total.** Add deductions on line 12, lines 15 and 16 in column (g), and lines 17 through 20. Enter here and on the appropriate lines of your return. Partnerships and S corporations—see instructions	21	2,672
22	For assets shown above and placed in service during the current year, enter the portion of the basis attributable to section 263A costs	22	

For Paperwork Reduction Act Notice, see the separate instructions. Cat. No. 12906N Form **4562** (1997)

Page 29

Appendix I: IRS Information

Form **1041** Department of the Treasury—Internal Revenue Service
U.S. Income Tax Return for Estates and Trusts 1997

For calendar year 1997 or fiscal year beginning , 1997, and ending , 19 | OMB No. 1545-0092

A Type of entity:
- ☑ Decedent's estate
- ☐ Simple trust
- ☐ Complex trust
- ☐ Grantor type trust
- ☐ Bankruptcy estate–Ch. 7
- ☐ Bankruptcy estate–Ch. 11
- ☐ Pooled income fund

B Number of Schedules K-1 attached (see instructions) ▶ 1

Name of estate or trust (If a grantor type trust, see page 7 of the instructions.)
Estate of John R. Smith

Name and title of fiduciary
Charles R. Smith, Executor

Number, street, and room or suite no. (If a P.O. box, see page 7 of the instructions.)
6406 Mayflower St.

City or town, state, and ZIP code
Juneville, ME 00000

C Employer identification number
10 : 0123456

D Date entity created
4-9-97

E Nonexempt charitable and split-interest trusts, check applicable boxes (see page 8 of the instructions):
- ☐ Described in section 4947(a)(1)
- ☐ Not a private foundation
- ☐ Described in section 4947(a)(2)

F Check applicable boxes: ☑ Initial return ☐ Final return ☐ Amended return ☐ Change in fiduciary's name ☐ Change in fiduciary's address

G Pooled mortgage account (see page 9 of the instructions): ☐ Bought ☐ Sold Date:

Section	Line	Description	Line	Amount
Income	1	Interest income	1	2,250
	2	Dividends	2	750
	3	Business income or (loss) (attach Schedule C or C-EZ (Form 1040))	3	
	4	Capital gain or (loss) (attach Schedule D (Form 1041))	4	200
	5	Rents, royalties, partnerships, other estates and trusts, etc. (attach Schedule E (Form 1040))	5	
	6	Farm income or (loss) (attach Schedule F (Form 1040))	6	
	7	Ordinary gain or (loss) (attach Form 4797)	7	
	8	Other income. List type and amount Salary and vacation pay	8	12,000
	9	**Total income.** Combine lines 1 through 8 ▶	9	15,200
Deductions	10	Interest. Check if Form 4952 is attached ▶ ☐	10	
	11	Taxes	11	2,250
	12	Fiduciary fees	12	
	13	Charitable deduction (from Schedule A, line 7)	13	
	14	Attorney, accountant, and return preparer fees	14	325
	15a	Other deductions NOT subject to the 2% floor (attach schedule)	15a	
	b	Allowable miscellaneous itemized deductions subject to the 2% floor	15b	
	16	**Total.** Add lines 10 through 15b	16	2,575
	17	Adjusted total income or (loss). Subtract line 16 from line 9. Enter here and on Schedule B, line 1 ▶	17	12,625
	18	Income distribution deduction (from Schedule B, line 15) (attach Schedules K-1 (Form 1041))	18	2,000
	19	Estate tax deduction (including certain generation-skipping taxes) (attach computation)	19	
	20	Section 1202 exclusion (see instructions)	20	
	21	Exemption	21	600
	22	**Total deductions.** Add lines 18 through 21 ▶	22	2,600
Tax and Payments	23	Taxable income. Subtract line 22 from line 17. If a loss, see page 13 of the instructions	23	10,025
	24	**Total tax** (from Schedule G, line 8)	24	3,026
	25	**Payments: a** 1997 estimated tax payments and amount applied from 1996 return	25a	
	b	Estimated tax payments allocated to beneficiaries (from Form 1041-T)	25b	
	c	Subtract line 25b from line 25a	25c	
	d	Tax paid with extension of time to file: ☐ Form 2758 ☐ Form 8736 ☐ Form 8800	25d	
	e	Federal income tax withheld. If any is from Form(s) 1099, check ▶ ☐	25e	
		Other payments: **f** Form 2439 ; **g** Form 4136 ; Total ▶	25h	
	26	**Total payments.** Add lines 25c through 25e, and 25h ▶	26	
	27	Estimated tax penalty (see page 13 of the instructions)	27	
	28	**Tax due.** If line 26 is smaller than the total of lines 24 and 27, enter amount owed	28	3,026
	29	**Overpayment.** If line 26 is larger than the total of lines 24 and 27, enter amount overpaid	29	
	30	Amount of line 29 to be: **a Credited to 1998 estimated tax** ▶ ; **b Refunded** ▶	30	

Please Sign Here

Under penalties of perjury, I declare that I have examined this return, including accompanying schedules and statements, and to the best of my knowledge and belief, it is true, correct, and complete. Declaration of preparer (other than fiduciary) is based on all information of which preparer has any knowledge.

▶ Charles R Smith, Executor | 3/24/98 | ▶
Signature of fiduciary or officer representing fiduciary | Date | EIN of fiduciary if a financial institution (see page 4 of the instructions)

Paid Preparer's Use Only

Preparer's signature ▶ | Date | Check if self-employed ☐ | Preparer's social security no.

Firm's name (or yours if self-employed) and address ▶ | EIN ▶ | ZIP code ▶

For Paperwork Reduction Act Notice, see the separate instructions. Cat. No. 11370H Form **1041** (1997)

Page 30

Form 1041 (1997) Page **2**

Schedule A **Charitable Deduction.** Do not complete for a simple trust or a pooled income fund.

1	Amounts paid or permanently set aside for charitable purposes from gross income (see instructions)	1	
2	Tax-exempt income allocable to charitable contributions (see page 14 of the instructions)	2	
3	Subtract line 2 from line 1	3	
4	Capital gains for the tax year allocated to corpus and paid or permanently set aside for charitable purposes	4	
5	Add lines 3 and 4	5	
6	Section 1202 exclusion allocable to capital gains paid or permanently set aside for charitable purposes (see instructions)	6	
7	**Charitable deduction.** Subtract line 6 from 5. Enter here and on page 1, line 13	7	

Schedule B **Income Distribution Deduction**

1	Adjusted total income (from page 1, line 17) (see page 14 of the instructions)	1	12,625
2	Adjusted tax-exempt interest	2	
3	Total net gain from Schedule D (Form 1041), line 17, column (1) (see page 15 of the instructions)	3	
4	Enter amount from Schedule A, line 4	4	
5	Capital gains for the tax year included on Schedule A, line 1	5	
6	Enter any gain from page 1, line 4, as a negative number. If page 1, line 4, is a loss, enter the loss as a positive number	6	(200)
7	**Distributable net income (DNI).** Combine lines 1 through 6. If zero or less, enter -0-	7	12,425
8	If a complex trust, enter accounting income for the tax year as determined under the governing instrument and applicable local law — 8		
9	Income required to be distributed currently	9	
10	Other amounts paid, credited, or otherwise required to be distributed	10	2,000
11	Total distributions. Add lines 9 and 10. If greater than line 8, see page 15 of the instructions	11	2,000
12	Enter the amount of tax-exempt income included on line 11	12	
13	Tentative income distribution deduction. Subtract line 12 from line 11	13	2,000
14	Tentative income distribution deduction. Subtract line 2 from line 7. If zero or less, enter -0-	14	12,425
15	**Income distribution deduction.** Enter the smaller of line 13 or line 14 here and on page 1, line 18	15	2,000

Schedule G **Tax Computation** (see page 16 of the instructions)

1	**Tax:** a ☐ Tax rate schedule or ☑ Schedule D (Form 1041)	1a	3,026		
	b Other taxes	1b			
	c Total. Add lines 1a and 1b ▶			1c	3,026
2a	Foreign tax credit (attach Form 1116)	2a			
b	Check: ☐ Nonconventional source fuel credit ☐ Form 8834	2b			
c	General business credit. Enter here and check which forms are attached: ☐ Form 3800 or ☐ Forms (specify) ▶	2c			
d	Credit for prior year minimum tax (attach Form 8801)	2d			
3	**Total credits.** Add lines 2a through 2d ▶			3	
4	Subtract line 3 from line 1c			4	3,026
5	Recapture taxes. Check if from: ☐ Form 4255 ☐ Form 8611			5	
6	Alternative minimum tax (from Schedule I, line 42)			6	-0-
7	Household employment taxes. Attach Schedule H (Form 1040)			7	
8	**Total tax.** Add lines 4 through 7. Enter here and on page 1, line 24 ▶			8	3,026

Other Information

		Yes	No
1	Did the estate or trust receive tax-exempt income? If "Yes," attach a computation of the allocation of expenses. Enter the amount of tax-exempt interest income and exempt-interest dividends ▶ $		✓
2	Did the estate or trust receive all or any part of the earnings (salary, wages, and other compensation) of any individual by reason of a contract assignment or similar arrangement?		✓
3	At any time during calendar year 1997, did the estate or trust have an interest in or a signature or other authority over a bank, securities, or other financial account in a foreign country? See page 17 of the instructions for exceptions and filing requirements for Form TD F 90-22.1. If "Yes," enter the name of the foreign country ▶		✓
4	During the tax year, did the estate or trust receive a distribution from, or was it the grantor of, or transferor to, a foreign trust? If "Yes," see page 17 of the instructions for other forms the estate or trust may have to file		✓
5	Did the estate or trust receive, or pay, any seller-financed mortgage interest? If "Yes," see page 17 for required attachment		✓
6	If this is an estate or a complex trust making the section 663(b) election, check here (see page 17) ▶ ☐		
7	To make a section 643(e)(3) election, attach Schedule D (Form 1041), and check here (see page 17) ▶ ☐		
8	If the decedent's estate has been open for more than 2 years, check here ▶ ☐		
9	Are any trust beneficiaries skip persons? See instructions		✓

Page 31

Schedule I **Alternative Minimum Tax** (see pages 18 through 22 of the instructions)

Part I—Estate's or Trust's Share of Alternative Minimum Taxable Income

1	Adjusted total income or (loss) (from page 1, line 17)			1	12,625
2	Net operating loss deduction. Enter as a positive amount			2	
3	Add lines 1 and 2			3	12,625
4	Adjustments and tax preference items:				
a	Interest	4a			
b	Taxes	4b	2,250		
c	Miscellaneous itemized deductions (from page 1, line 15b)	4c			
d	Refund of taxes	4d	( )		
e	Depreciation of property placed in service after 1986	4e			
f	Circulation and research and experimental expenditures	4f			
g	Mining exploration and development costs	4g			
h	Long-term contracts entered into after February 28, 1986	4h			
i	Amortization of pollution control facilities	4i			
j	Installment sales of certain property	4j			
k	Adjusted gain or loss (including incentive stock options)	4k			
l	Certain loss limitations	4l			
m	Tax shelter farm activities	4m			
n	Passive activities	4n			
o	Beneficiaries of other trusts or decedent's estates	4o			
p	Tax-exempt interest from specified private activity bonds	4p			
q	Depletion	4q			
r	Accelerated depreciation of real property placed in service before 1987	4r			
s	Accelerated depreciation of leased personal property placed in service before 1987	4s			
t	Intangible drilling costs	4t			
u	Other adjustments	4u			
5	Combine lines 4a through 4u			5	2,250
6	Add lines 3 and 5			6	14,875
7	Alternative tax net operating loss deduction (see page 21 of the instructions for limitations)			7	
8	Adjusted alternative minimum taxable income. Subtract line 7 from line 6. Enter here and on line 14 **Note:** *Complete Part II below before going to line 9.*			8	14,875
9	Income distribution deduction from line 28	9	2,000		
10	Estate tax deduction (from page 1, line 19)	10			
11	Multiply the section 1202 exclusion from page 1, line 20, by 58% (.58)	11			
12	Add lines 9 through 11			12	2,000
13	Estate's or trust's share of alternative minimum taxable income. Subtract line 12 from line 8			13	12,875

If line 13 is:

- $22,500 or less, stop here and enter -0- on Schedule G, line 6. The estate or trust is not liable for the alternative minimum tax.
- Over $22,500, but less than $165,000, go to line 29.
- $165,000 or more, enter the amount from line 13 on line 35 and go to line 36.

(continued on page 4)

Form 1041 (1996) Page **4**

Part II—Income Distribution Deduction on a Minimum Tax Basis

14	Adjusted alternative minimum taxable income (from line 8)	14	14,875
15	Adjusted tax-exempt interest (other than amounts included on line 4p)	15	
16	Total net gain from Schedule D (Form 1041), line 17, column (1). If a loss, enter -0-	16	
17	Capital gains for the tax year allocated to corpus and paid or permanently set aside for charitable purposes (from Schedule A, line 4)	17	
18	Capital gains paid or permanently set aside for charitable purposes from gross income (see page 21 of the instructions)	18	
19	Capital gains computed on a minimum tax basis included on line 8	19	(200)
20	Capital losses computed on a minimum tax basis included on line 8. Enter as a positive amount	20	
21	Distributable net alternative minimum taxable income (DNAMTI). Combine lines 14 through 20. If zero or less, enter -0-	21	14,675
22	Income required to be distributed currently (from Schedule B, line 9)	22	
23	Other amounts paid, credited, or otherwise required to be distributed (from Schedule B, line 10)	23	2,000
24	Total distributions. Add lines 22 and 23	24	2,000
25	Tax-exempt income included on line 24 (other than amounts included on line 4p)	25	
26	Tentative income distribution deduction on a minimum tax basis. Subtract line 25 from line 24	26	2,000
27	Tentative income distribution deduction on a minimum tax basis. Subtract line 15 from line 21. If zero or less, enter -0-	27	14,675
28	**Income distribution deduction on a minimum tax basis.** Enter the smaller of line 26 or line 27. Enter here and on line 9	28	2,000

Part III—Alternative Minimum Tax

29	Exemption amount			29	$22,500
30	Enter the amount from line 13	30			
31	Phase-out of exemption amount	31	$75,000		
32	Subtract line 31 from line 30. If zero or less, enter -0-	32			
33	Multiply line 32 by 25% (.25)			33	
34	Subtract line 33 from line 29. If zero or less, enter -0-			34	
35	Subtract line 34 from line 30			35	
36	If you completed Schedule D (Form 1041) and had an amount on line 28 or 35 (as refigured for the AMT, if necessary), go to Part IV to figure line 36. **All others:** If line 35 is— • $175,000 or less, multiply line 35 by 26% (.26). • Over $175,000, multiply line 35 by 28% (.28) and subtract $3,500 from the result			36	
37	Alternative minimum foreign tax credit (see page 21 of instructions)			37	
38	Tentative minimum tax. Subtract line 37 from line 36			38	
39	Regular tax before credits (see page 22 of instructions)	39			
40	Section 644 tax included on Schedule G, line 1b	40			
41	Add lines 39 and 40			41	
42	**Alternative minimum tax.** Subtract line 41 from line 38. If zero or less, enter -0-. Enter here and on Schedule G, line 6			42	

 *Printed on recycled paper*

SCHEDULE D (Form 1041)
Department of the Treasury
Internal Revenue Service

Capital Gains and Losses

▶ Attach to Form 1041 (or Form 5227). See the separate instructions for Form 1041 (or Form 5227).

OMB No. 1545-0092
1997

Name of estate or trust: Estate of John R. Smith
Employer identification number: 10 : 0123456

Note: *Form 5227 filers need to complete ONLY Parts I and II.*

Part I Short-Term Capital Gains and Losses—Assets Held One Year or Less

	(a) Description of property (Example, 100 shares 7% preferred of "Z" Co.)	(b) Date acquired (mo., day, yr.)	(c) Date sold (mo., day, yr.)	(d) Sales price	(e) Cost or other basis (see instructions)	(f) Gain or (loss) for entire year. (col. (d) less col. (e))
1						

		Line	(f)
2	Short-term capital gain or (loss) from Forms 4684, 6252, 6781, and 8824	2	
3	Net short-term gain or (loss) from partnerships, S corporations, and other estates or trusts	3	
4	Short-term capital loss carryover from 1996 Schedule D, line 28	4	( )
5	**Net short-term gain or (loss).** Combine lines 1 through 4 in column (f). Enter here and on line 14 below ▶	5	

Part II Long-Term Capital Gains and Losses—Assets Held More Than One Year

	(a) Description of property (Example, 100 shares 7% preferred of "Z" Co.)	(b) Date acquired (mo., day, yr.)	(c) Date sold (mo., day, yr.)	(d) Sales price	(e) Cost or other basis (see instructions)	(f) Gain or (loss) for entire year. (col. (d) less col. (e))	(g) 28% rate gain or (loss) *(see instr. below)
6	Coin Collection	4-9-97	9-22-97	3,000	2,800	200	200

		Line	(f)	(g)
7	Long-term capital gain or (loss) from Forms 2439, 4684, 6252, 6781, and 8824	7		
8	Net long-term gain or (loss) from partnerships, S corporations, and other estates or trusts	8		
9	Capital gain distributions	9		
10	Gain from Form 4797	10		
11	Long-term capital loss carryover from 1996 Schedule D, line 35	11	( )	
12	Combine lines 6 through 11 in column (g)	12		200
13	**Net long-term gain or (loss).** Combine lines 6 through 12 in column (f). Enter here and on line 15 below ▶	13	200	

*28% rate gain or loss includes all gains and losses from Part II, column (f) from sales, exchanges, or conversions (including installment payments recieved) **either:**

- **Before** May 7, 1997, **or**
- **After** July 28, 1997, for assets that were held more than 1 year but **not** more than 18 months.

It also includes ALL "collectibles gains and losses" (as defined on page 23 of the instructions).

Part III Summary of Parts I and II

		Line	(1) Beneficiaries' (see instructions)	(2) Estate's or trust's	(3) Total
14	**Net short-term gain or (loss)**	14			
15	**Net long-term gain or (loss):**				
	a 28% rate gain or (loss) (from line 12 above)	15a		200	200
	b Unrecaptured section 1250 gain (see instructions)	15b			
	c Total for year (from line 13 above)	15c		200	200
16	**Total net gain or (loss).** Combine lines 14 and 16c ▶	16		200	200

Note: *If line 16, column (3), is a net gain, enter the gain on Form 1041, line 4. If lines 15c and 16, column (2) are net gains, go to Part V, and DO NOT complete Part IV. If line 16, column (3), is a net loss, complete Part IV and the* ***Capital Loss Carryover Worksheet,*** *as necessary.*

For Paperwork Reduction Act Notice, see the Instructions for Form 1041. Cat. No. 11376V **Schedule D (Form 1041) 1997**

Page 34

Part IV Capital Loss Limitation

17	Enter here and enter as a (loss) on Form 1041, line 4, the smaller of: a The loss on line 16, column (3); **or** b $3,000	17	( )

If the loss on line 16, column (3) is more than $3,000, OR if Form 1041, page 1, line 23, is a loss, complete the Capital Loss Carryover Worksheet in the instructions to determine your capital loss carryover.

Part V Tax Computation Using Maximum Capital Gains Rates (Complete this part only if both lines 15c and 16, column (2) are gains, and Form 1041, line 23 is more than zero.)

18	Enter taxable income from Form 1041, line 23			18	10,025
19	Enter the **smaller** of line 15c or 16, column (2)	19	200		
20	If you are filing Form 4952, enter the amount from Form 4952, line 4e	20			
21	Subtract line 20 from line 19. If zero or less, enter -0-	21	200		
22	Combine lines 14 and 15a, column (2). If zero or less, enter -0-	22	200		
23	Enter the **smaller** of line 15a, column (2), or line 22, but not less than zero	23	200		
24	Enter the amount from line 15b, column (2) (see instructions)	24			
25	Enter the amount from Form 1041, line 20, if any	25			
26	Add lines 23 through 25	26	200		
27	Subtract line 26 from line 21. If zero or less, enter -0-			27	–0–
28	Subtract line 27 from line 18. If zero or less, enter -0-			28	10,025
29	Enter the **smaller** of line 18 or $1,650			29	1,650
30	Enter the **smaller** of line 28 or line 29			30	1,650
31	Subtract line 21 from line 18. If zero or less, enter -0-			31	9,825
32	Enter the **larger** of line 30 or line 31			32	9,825
33	Tax on amount on line 32 from the 1997 Tax Rate Schedule ▶			33	2,970
34	Enter the amount from line 29			34	1,650
35	Enter the amount from line 28			35	10,025
36	Subtract line 35 from line 34. If zero or less, enter -0-			36	–0–
37	Multiply line 36 by 10% (.10) ▶			37	–0–
38	Enter the **smaller** of line 18 or line 27			38	–0–
39	Enter the amount from line 36.			39	–0–
40	Subtract line 39 from line 38. If zero or less, enter -0-			40	–0–
41	Multiply line 40 by 20% (.20) ▶			41	–0–
42	Enter the **smaller** of line 21 or line 24			42	–0–
43	Add lines 21 and 32	43	10,025		
44	Enter the amount from line 18	44	10,025		
45	Subtract line 44 from line 43. If zero or less, enter -0-			45	–0–
46	Subtract line 45 from line 42. If zero or less, enter -0-			46	–0–
47	Multiply line 46 by 25% (.25) ▶			47	–0–
48	Enter the amount from line 18			48	10,025
49	Add lines 32, 36, 40, and 46			49	9,825
50	Subtract line 49 from line 48			50	200
51	Multiply line 50 by 28% (.28) ▶			51	56
52	Add lines 33, 37, 41, 47, and 51			52	3,026
53	Tax on the amount on line 18 from the 1997 Tax Rate Schedule			53	3,049
54	Tax. Enter the **smaller** of line 52 or line 53 here and on line 1a of Schedule G, Form 1041 ▶			54	3,026

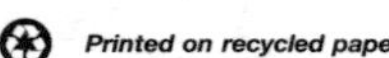

SCHEDULE K-1 (Form 1041)

Department of the Treasury
Internal Revenue Service

Beneficiary's Share of Income, Deductions, Credits, etc.

for the calendar year 1997, or fiscal year
beginning ...., 1997, ending ...., 19 ......
► Complete a separate Schedule K-1 for each beneficiary.

OMB No. 1545-0092

1997

☐ Amended K-1
☐ Final K-1

Name of trust or decedent's estate
Estate of John R. Smith

Beneficiary's identifying number ► 123-00-6789

Estate's or trust's EIN ► 10 : 0123456

Beneficiary's name, address, and ZIP code
James Smith
6407 Mayflower Street
Juneville, ME 00000

Fiduciary's name, address, and ZIP code
Charles R. Smith, Executor
6406 Mayflower Street
Juneville, ME 00000

(a) Allocable share item		(b) Amount	(c) Calendar year 1997 Form 1040 filers enter the amounts in column (b) on:
1 Interest	1	300	Schedule B, Part I, line 1
2 Dividends	2	100	Schedule B, Part II, line 5
3 Net short-term capital gain	3a		Schedule D, line 5, column (f)
4 Net long-term capital gain: a 28% rate gain	4a		Schedule D, line 13, column (g)
b unrecaptured section 1250 gain	4b		See the instructions for Schedule D, line 25
c Total for year	4c		Schedule D, line 13, column (f)
5a Annuities, royalties, and other nonpassive income before directly apportioned deductions	5a	1,600	Schedule E, Part III, column (f)
b Depreciation	5b		Include on the applicable line of the appropriate tax form
c Depletion	5c		
d Amortization	5d		
6a Trade or business, rental real estate, and other rental income before directly apportioned deductions (see instructions)	6a		Schedule E, Part III
b Depreciation	6b		Include on the applicable line of the appropriate tax form
c Depletion	6c		
d Amortization	6d		
7 Income for minimum tax purposes	7	2,000	
8 Income for regular tax purposes (add lines 1, 2, 3b, 4b, 5a, and 6a)	8	2,000	
9 Adjustment for minimum tax purposes (subtract line 8 from line 7)	9		Form 6251, line 12
10 Estate tax deduction (including certain generation-skipping transfer taxes)	10		Schedule A, line 27
11 Foreign taxes	11		Form 1116 or Schedule A (Form 1040), line 8
12 Adjustments and tax preference items (itemize):			
a Accelerated depreciation	12a		Include on the applicable line of Form 6251
b Depletion	12b		
c Amortization	12c		
d Exclusion items	12d		1998 Form 8801
13 Deductions in the final year of trust or decedent's estate:			
a Excess deductions on termination (see instructions)	13a		Schedule A, line 22
b Short-term capital loss carryover	13b		Schedule D, line 5, column (f)
c Long-term capital loss carryover	13c		Schedule D, line 13, column (f)
d Net operating loss (NOL) carryover for regular tax purposes	13d		Form 1040, line 21
e NOL carryover for minimum tax purposes	13e		See the instructions for Form 6251, line 20
f	13f		Include on the applicable line of the appropriate tax form
g	13g		
14 Other (itemize):			
a Payments of estimated taxes credited to you	14a		Form 1040, line 55
b Tax-exempt interest	14b		Form 1040, line 8b
c	14c		Include on the applicable line of the appropriate tax form
d	14d		
e	14e		
f	14f		
g	14g		
h	14h		

For Paperwork Reduction Act Notice, see the Instructions for Form 1041. Cat. No. 11380D **Schedule K-1 (Form 1041) 1997**

Page 36

Table A. **Checklist of Forms and Due Dates—For Executor, Administrator, or Personal Representative**

Form No.	Title	Due Date
SS-4	Application for Employer Identification Number	As soon as possible. The identification number must be included in returns, statements, and other documents.
56	Notice Concerning Fiduciary Relationship	As soon as all of the necessary information is available.*
706	United States Estate (and Generation-Skipping Transfer) Tax Return	9 months after date of decedent's death.
706-A	United States Additional Estate Tax Return	6 months after cessation or disposition of special-use valuation property.
706-CE	Certificate of Payment of Foreign Death Tax	9 months after decedent's death. To be filed with Form 706.
706-GS(D)	Generation-Skipping Transfer Tax Return for Distributions	See form instructions.
706-GS(D-1)	Notification of Distribution From A Generation-Skipping Trust	See form instructions.
706-GS(T)	Generation-Skipping Transfer Tax Return for Terminations	See form instructions.
706-NA	United States Estate (and Generation-Skipping Transfer) Tax Return, Estate of nonresident not a citizen of the United States	9 months after date of decedent's death.
712	Life Insurance Statement	Part I to be filed with estate tax return.
1040	U.S. Individual Income Tax Return	Generally, April 15th of the year after death.
1040NR	U.S. Nonresident Alien Income Tax Return	See form instructions.
1041	U.S. Income Tax Return for Estates and Trusts	15th day of 4th month after end of estate's tax eyar.
1041-A	U.S. Information Return—Trust Accumulation of Charitable Amounts	April 15th.
1041-T	Allocation of Estimated Tax Payments to Beneficiaries	March 6th.
1041-ES	Estimated Income Tax for Estates and Trusts	Generally, April 15, June 15, Sept. 15, and Jan. 15 for calendar-year filers.
1042	Annual Withholding Tax Return for U.S. Source Income of Foreign Persons	March 15th.
1042-S	Foreign Person's U.S. Source Income Subject to Withholding	March 15th.
1310	Statement of Person Claiming Refund Due a Deceased Taxpayer	To be filed with Form 1040, Form 1040A, Form 1040EZ, or Form 1040NR if refund is due.
2758	Application for Extension of Time To File Certain Excise, Income, Information, and Other Returns	Sufficiently early to permit IRS to consider the application and reply before the due date of Form 1041.
4768	Application for Extension of Time To File a Return and/or Pay U.S. Estate (and Generation-Skipping Transfer) Taxes	Sufficiently early to permit IRS to consider the application and reply before the estate tax due date.
4810	Request for Prompt Assessment Under Internal Revenue Code Section 6501(d)	As soon as possible after filing Form 1040 or Form 1041.
5495	Request for Discharge from Personal Liability Under Internal Revenue Code Section 6905	After filing the returns listed on this form.
8300	Report of Cash Payments Over $10,000 Received in a Trade or Business	15th day after the date of the transaction.
8822	Change of Address	As soon as the address is changed.

* A personal representative must report the termination of the estate, in writing, to the Internal Revenue Service. Form 56 may be used for this purpose.

Page 37

Table B. **Worksheet to Reconcile Amounts Reported in Name of Decedent on Information Forms (Forms W-2, 1099-INT, 1099-DIV, Etc.) (Please Keep This for Your Records)**

Name of Decedent	Date of Death	Decedent's Social Security Number
Name of Personal Representative, Executor, or Administrator		**Estate's Employer Identification Number (If Any)**

Source (list each payer)	A Enter total amount shown on information form	B Enter part of amount in Column A reportable on decedent's final return	C Amount reportable on estate's or beneficiary's income tax return (Column A minus Column B)	D Portion of Column C that is "Income in respect of a decedent"
1. Wages				
2. Interest income				
3. Dividends				
4. State income tax refund				
5. Capital gains				
6. Pension income				
7. Rents, royalties				
8. Taxes withheld*				
9. Other items, such as: social security, business and farm income or loss, unemployment compensation, etc.				

* List each withholding agent (employer, etc.)

Page 38

Index

Appendix II
Estate Planning Information

The Secret Millionaire Series:

The Secret Millionaire Guide To Nevada Corporations
The Secret Millionaire Guide To Living Trusts
The Secret Millionaire Guide To Pension Plans
The Secret Millionaire Audio Tape Set on Nevada Corporations
The Secret Millionaire Demo CD-Rom on Nevada Corporation Maintenance

Seminars available from Wade Cook Seminars, Inc. (1-800-872-7411)

BEST™—Business and Entity Skills Training
Wealth Institute

Entities available from Entity Planners, Inc. (1-800-706-4741)

Nevada Corporations
Living Trusts
Pension Plans
Limited Partnerships
Charitable Remainder Trusts

Million Heirs

Million Heirs Resource Kits available from Vantage Planners, LLC (1-888-338-9264)

Million Heirs Demo CD-Rom

This powerful new software package shows you how to document important legal, personal, and financial information in order to protect your family's assets.

Million Heirs Mastery Video

In this dynamic video, a group of leading experts discuss effective strategies for taking care of your million heirs.

Million Heir Money Secret Audio Cassette

The exciting discussion of strategies used to maintain a working knowledge of your family's finances.

To order one of the resource kits above, call 1-888-338-9264 and ask for offer code MHB, or visit www.secretmillionaire.com.